PERIOD HOUSES

For John and Roger, Anne, Frank, Malcolm and Susan,
and all my friends who worked in the Greater London Council's
Historic Buildings Division

In memory of Blanche

PERIOD HOUSES

ANTHONY QUINEY

A GUIDE TO AUTHENTIC ARCHITECTURAL FEATURES

GEORGE
PHILIP

Introduction

At a rough estimate there are between two and three million houses surviving in Britain from before the First World War. These are the subject of this book. All their features are explained, starting with the houses which served medieval yeomen and ending with those which served Edwardian traders. So, everything is here, from the medieval hall to the Edwardian dado. Understand its context, and a house becomes living history, worthy of care, not just expenditure. Indeed care enlightened by understanding may even save expense.

About twenty years ago, when I was working in the Historic Buildings Division of the Greater London Council, we were confronted with a tenant of a farm in the GLC's ownership who wanted a new house. Blanche Farm was timber framed and weatherboarded, and dated from the sixteenth century, but a lack of proper maintenance for many years had left it leaky, cold and sub-standard. Complete repair was estimated to cost £17,000, a new house £11,000. So, despite its age and being listed for its special architectural and historic interest, it was demolished. So passed Blanche Farm.

Sadly for the GLC, the cost of the new house turned out to be far in excess of the quoted £11,000, and the cost of repairing the old house, it turned out later, could have been greatly cut. One aim of this book is that such treatment of period houses should not be ignorantly repeated. Care stems from appreciation, and my purpose is therefore to increase the reader's — and especially the house owner's — appreciation of all the various surviving houses which have served the needs of ordinary people during the last eight centuries.

Published in 1989 by George Philip Limited
59 Grosvenor Street, London W1X 9DA

British Library Cataloguing in Publication Data

Quiney, Anthony
    Discovering period houses: guide to restoration
    1. Dwellings—Great Britain—Maintenance and
    repair 2. Dwellings—Great Britain—Remodelling
    I. Title
    728'.028'8   TH4817

ISBN 0-540-01173-8

Contents

Two faces of the period house: stone and thatch in a seventeenth-century house at Sulgrave, Northamptonshire; timber, lath and plaster, and tile (BELOW) in a fifteenth-century house at Cuxton, Kent. Both have been altered and extended over the years for the sake of convenience, but neither has departed so far from its origins as to be unrecognizable.

Period houses

T his Goodhurst I went to', wrote the indefatigable traveller Celia Fiennes in
1697, 'its a pretty large place, old timber houses, but' – and here she
referred to their occupants – 'they are a sort of yeomanly Gentry, about 2
or 3 or 400£ a year and eate and drink well and live comfortably and hospitably . . . .'

She was writing of the most prosperous of England's peasantry, the yeomen who
inhabited much of Kent, not just the township of Goudhurst. These people had kept
their freedom throughout the Middle Ages and consequently had been able to profit
from combining arable and pastoral farming with tanning and weaving, and later
with cultivating hops and fruit. This had made them affluent, in fact so affluent that
to call them peasants stretches the term to breaking point. They formed an incipient
middle class, one that was proverbially richer than some of the gentry or even the
lesser aristocracy of poorer parts of the country such as Cornwall or the north
country. Celia Fiennes saw the most visible evidence of their wealth in their fine old
houses. Between the middle of the fourteenth century and the middle of the
sixteenth, they had built themselves so many well-constructed and capacious houses
that these were still serving them some two centuries later when she travelled
through Kent. They still serve today, and many of them are instantly recognizable.
Indeed, nowhere else in all Europe is there so great a concentration of medieval
peasant houses as here.

One conclusion to be drawn from this is that living in what estate agents now call
a period house is not a new fashion. You may need to be comparatively affluent to do
so, but you do not need to be ostentatiously rich. The yeomen of Kent were well
known for the modesty of their dress and even a degree of puritanism, and, in a sense,
this showed in their willingness to stick to the old values enshrined in their houses. In
the course of time, they modernized their houses to take advantage of such
innovations as glazed windows and enclosed hearths with chimney-stacks. Without
this modernization their houses would eventually have failed to satisfy even the most
basic standards of later ages. That far the yeomen of Kent were little different from us
today. Would we, after all, keep electricity out of our houses just because they were
built long before it became available for domestic consumption?

More importantly, what the yeomen of Kent had achieved with their house-
building at the end of the Middle Ages was the start of a wider change that brought
substantial, well-built houses to at least half the population by the end of the
seventeenth century. What the yeomen of Kent achieved was also a small revolution
in their own time. They were the first widespread group of peasants rich enough to

use new techniques of carpentry, which had been developed in the twelfth and thirteenth centuries, on a large scale. These techniques made it possible to build a house that would last indefinitely, because carpenters could erect its timber frame with such secure joints that there was no need of support from posts set into the ground. The frame could therefore be built entirely on a more or less dry plinth, ensuring that it would not easily rot.

Because of the assiduous cultivation of oak in many parts of the country, carpenters could build houses of this finest of all British hardwoods, and they would last indefinitely if properly maintained. The evidence can be seen in hundreds of English villages from Worsbrough in Yorkshire, across to Weobley in Herefordshire and down to Wye in Kent. In fact there are probably very few villages in Kent without at least one medieval timber-framed house, even though it may lie buried beneath the accretions of later years. Despite this record, there is no reason to believe that medieval house-carpenters expected that their houses would last so long; but it is a matter of some reproach that modern builders, with all their industrial products, hardly expect their houses to last one century, let alone five.

Now that a house did not need to be rebuilt every generation, as nearly all peasant houses had had to be beforehand, there was a sound reason for maintaining it. Celia Fiennes found this remarkable, not just for its own sake, but because, with so many substantial old houses in Kent, there was little need for new ones – and it showed.

Goudhurst, looking up the hill towards Church House, a sixteenth-century house Celia Fiennes must have seen. Its timber frame has now been hung with tiles and several additions have been made to it. Nevertheless, its original form is still clear and its overall appearance has not changed so much since her time.

A late sixteenth-century house at Kirdford in the West Sussex Weald, built with a timber frame whose major elements had been developed three hundred years beforehand, but whose decoration, with walls divided up into a series of small rectangular panels, was comparatively new at the time. Within a century, though, timber framing was falling out of use because, in this part of England, brick had become cheaper. The roof is covered with local sandstone tiles.

This frame of a house at Boxted, Essex, is one of the oldest yet recognized in England. It was probably built in the middle of the thirteenth century at a time when house builders were developing their techniques of carpentry far enough to allow a timber frame to need no support from earth-fast posts. Instead, the main uprights were placed on a plinth, and the rest of the frame braced them upright. This marks the start of the first revolution in the development of the English home, because it gave a house for the first time an indefinite life span if properly maintained. The arrangement of rooms, on the other hand, was not new. Most of this house consists of an open hall, already a traditional feature going back several centuries. Here a fire burnt on an open hearth and the smoke drifted up to disperse through the roof. For the rest, a service room where food was stored and a chamber over it for sleeping completed the accommodation.

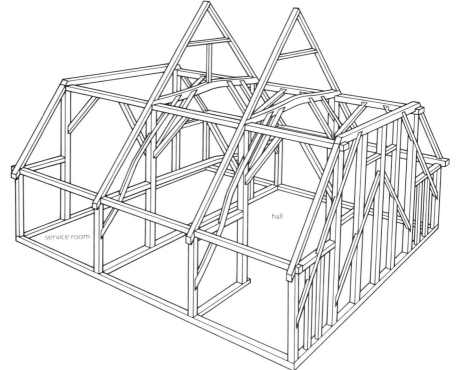

Two sixteenth-century timber-framed houses, in different parts of the country, one in Kent, the other in Herefordshire. In both of these counties oak was plentiful, and this is demonstrated in the prolific use of decorative studding. Each of the two houses was built with an enclosed chimney-stack, thus marking the second revolution in the development of the English house, which made it possible to dispense with a traditional open hall.

The house at Bredwardine, Herefordshire (BELOW), has the characteristically decorated gables of the west Midlands. Lower parts of the house are built of stone, which was coming within the reach of increasingly affluent yeoman builders.

The house at Lynsted, Kent (BOTTOM), has typical close-studding and a jetty from end to end to show on the outside its continuous upper floor.

The question of renovation

The present debate about whether it is more economic to maintain old houses and rehabilitate them if necessary or to demolish them and build new ones begs several questions. For a start, how far can an old house be valued above a modern equivalent, and how far do its limitations interfere with the amenities brought by modern technology? Another difficulty is how one should compare a house largely made by hand, at a time when skilled labour was comparatively cheap, with a modern house largely made from industrially manufactured parts.

Unlike motor cars, where several overwhelming advantages accrue from the most modern processes, houses can be adapted to keep them up to date in most important ways, yet still retain a large degree of their original character. This has an emotional value: people without history are like people without memory, and old houses are one of the most potent visible reminders of the past and its continuity with the present. Putting aside whatever emotional value this has, there is also a monetary value, if only through a never-ending demand for old houses that is reflected in their prices. This need for a link with the past can also be valued to some extent in the provision of the 'period' styling that marks so many brand-new houses.

This concern for the past is not a recent development. Even medieval houses used already ancient decorative features, such as embattled parapets, as romantic reminders of a past age. Today, the immense changes of the twentieth century's scientific revolution have served only to increase this need to keep in touch with the past. Maybe it is just this that has brought about the use of reproduction historic features as the principal stylistic embellishment of some of today's domestic architecture. Nevertheless, these features satisfy a deep-seated need, solidly based on the recognition that people want continuity in their lives and therefore in the houses where they live. On the other hand, when this respect for the past leads to conserving traditional workmanship in old houses, it is not just fulfilling an emotional need, it is a sensible economic choice as well. Above all, it keeps the inheritance of the past secure to be handed down to future generations.

Revolutions in house design

For the most part the history of the English house is an account of progressive evolution. Houses always have been adapted to keep them up to date, and this process can be continued. There were, despite that, three major revolutions in its history. The first of these began in the thirteenth century when the new techniques of timber-framing made it possible for houses to survive from one generation to the next and, as a result, gave us the historic basis of today's housing stock. The second revolution began in the sixteenth century and brought about a far more comfortable house, principally through the provision of enclosed fireplaces set within chimney-stacks instead of open hearths, and windows that, instead of being mere openings, were filled with glass and kept out the weather. The last revolution began in the nineteenth century and brought modern services to the house, running water and mains drainage on the one hand, piped gas and electricity on the other.

All these revolutions changed the way people lived. The first freed people from the constant need of rebuilding and gave village and town alike an appearance that was not constantly changing in nearly all its aspects. The second brought radical changes to the form of the house, and the last added to them. Both of the latter revolutions affected the comfort of people's lives more than they affected their surroundings. Of course, the arrival of modern services also greatly reduced the amount of work needed to maintain a household.

A major consequence of the two later revolutions was to make the houses of the past obsolescent. Consequently existing houses were modified, some demolished. There is now another period of change which has introduced an expanding range of industrial materials to make house construction easier and save labour. These materials include concrete, plastics and prefabricated parts, all of which have undoubted advantages. For many an architect, these materials, together with the services brought about by the last revolution, have been tantamount to making old houses seem utterly redundant. That singular view found expression in the design of hundreds of thousands of new dwellings built after the Second World War, and has caused countless troubles ever since.

Where old houses are concerned, adaptation worked well enough in the seventeenth century, as Celia Fiennes saw, and there is plenty of evidence to show that it works well enough today. It does, though, need care. It needs care with the introduction or modernization of the services; it needs care with the repair and maintenance of the fabric of the house itself; and it needs care with the recognition and preservation of the historic features that give the house its individual character. These features are the special concern of this book.

The widespread desire to preserve the historic features of all kinds of buildings as well as houses has led to the conservation movement of the last few decades. One result has been increasing protection through law. Current historic buildings legislation makes it mandatory on any owner of a building statutorily listed for its special architectural or historic interest to gain 'listed building consent' before any building works are undertaken which might affect that interest. This applies whether the works are done inside the house or outside. It is a common fallacy that only the outsides of listed houses are protected in this way. It is also a common fallacy that no works can be undertaken to a listed house at all. So far as what can and what cannot be done to a particular listed building, there is always recourse to the conservation officer or the planning department of the local authority, and they can also give advice about houses that are not listed but are protected to a lesser degree because they lie within a conservation area.

The principles of conservation
Conservation officers are usually very busy people and there is much to be said for understanding what the principles of conservation are before seeking advice. This saves a house owner's time as well as the conservation officer's. Far more

importantly, a little understanding of these principles and what they are designed to protect increases one's appreciation of a house immeasurably. Moreover, these principles have a greater application than to listed houses alone, and can profitably be applied to any house. In this way its individual quality can be maintained, whatever it is, and in some cases it can be enhanced by careful restoration. Of course a sow's ear of a house cannot be made into a silken purse, but fewer houses than you imagine are so without any quality that they cannot be profitably rehabilitated.

There is some logic in undertaking this, and a lot of emotion. A well maintained house will keep its value better than a poorly maintained one, and a house with a complete range of period details is worth more than one without them. If the period details of a particular house do not please, it is better to buy a different house than change the details for new ones. Nothing looks worse to today's taste than a once proud house done up in a new style, not originally its own. The modernization of a Victorian terrace house, for instance, by covering over its multicoloured brickwork with fake stonework and exchanging its sash windows for double-glazed picture windows is an expensive way of ruining its character with no lasting benefit except to the suppliers of plastic stonework and double glazing. Conversely, to paint the brickwork white and exchange the plain sashes for small-paned bow windows in the hopes that the house will pass muster as a Georgian cottage is nearly as senseless. Admittedly, this is all a matter of taste, and consequently dangerous ground. The truth is that people have been altering their houses in the name of taste from the earliest times, and a Georgian façade thrown across a medieval frame is often viewed with pleasure today as it was when it was first done.

A moment's glance at any village or street of historic houses demonstrates that people cannot leave their houses alone. There would be nothing wrong with that if historic houses were not a wasting asset which cannot be replaced. The pace of change since the Second World War means that, if significant numbers of old houses are to survive, the past must be respected for what it was and an easy compromise needs to be achieved with the present. Energy put both into cleaning Victorian brickwork so that its true, fresh colours stand out, and into stripping generations of paint from stucco ornament so that its lines regain their original crisp outlines, is worth any amount of money spent on turning a house into something it never was. For that reason again, doing up a house with period ornament to give it a completeness it never had is to gild a lily, although people have been turning houses into something they never were and gilding them in the name of status from time immemorial. Even more absurd is to dress up the façade 'in the style of its time' and then gut the interior to provide all the amenities of a transatlantic hotel. Such a house would be better built from scratch. Nevertheless, the need for some change is unavoidable. We may not need a swimming pool behind our Georgian façade, but we do need a bathroom.

How far one should balance the unavoidable desire for change with the desire for continuity is a matter of individual preference. One thing is certain: however far the domestic architecture of the past is conserved, the past itself can never be recreated.

A house in period style, recently built at East Dean, East Sussex, though, for all its appeal to tradition, there is nothing about its design that belongs any more to Sussex than, say, to the Midlands. The timber-framing is, in any case, no more than applied to a block-work wall, and has no structural purpose. Nevertheless, it fills a deep need by maintaining a link with the past. This seems to have been a necessity since the time when the first houses were built permanently enough to last more than a generation or two. It continues today despite the effects of the industrial and scientific revolutions which have increased the comfort of today's houses beyond all recognition.

This house in Blackheath, London, is dated 1793 and has what appears to be decoration contemporary with such a date. In fact it was built in the late 1820s, and was one of the most attractive houses in its street. That was all in the past, for the false date and decoration were added in a recent rebuilding that reduced the old house to little more than a shell; the old decoration was replaced by a travesty of what it had before, and behind the façade there are now '2 magnificent swimming pools (one indoor), landscaped gardens with pond, enormous reception areas for impressive entertaining, library, 5 bedrooms, 5 bathrooms', all in a 'unique style'. The house is no doubt as desirable as its high asking price, but it would be just as desirable if it were entirely new and built elsewhere; then, at least, a good late Georgian house would not have been sacrificed.

There is no life in dead men's shoes. Conversely, once an old house has been changed out of all recognition it has gone for ever. With genuinely old houses becoming an increasing rarity, they become an ever more valuable document of the past, and it pays in all kinds of ways to respect them and to conserve the evidence of their history.

Probably half the houses in the United Kingdom were built before the Second World War, and half of these before 1914; so, when people move into a house that is new to them, they may well move into one that is already generations old, even if it is not centuries old. They may well have to choose between how far to modernize it and how far to conserve it, because the two processes are not always entirely compatible. This choice may have to respect the limits imposed by historic buildings legislation, but how skilfully this is achieved in any old house, whether or not it is listed, depends on an understanding of what that old house was once like. For that, it is necessary to know how it was planned, how it was built, and how it was decorated.

For the rich yeomen of Kent, a house principally consisted of a hall. Since at least the seventh century, English kings had built halls as communal rooms for banqueting and holding court. Manorial lords built lesser halls for a similar purpose; and so did the more prosperous yeomen, though for them banqueting and holding court meant little more than eating their everyday meals and planning their farming activities with their families and the servants who made up their households.

The principal feature of a hall was that it had a hearth somewhere in the middle, and, since there was no chimney-stack, it was open to the roof to allow the smoke to escape. This was its main distinguishing feature; today, it is often the remains of soot from that fire, still to be found on the old roof rafters, that provide the first recognizable evidence for the existence of a formerly open hall beneath. The hall was the largest part of a house, again a distinguishing feature, and height and size generally were objects conferring esteem on the owner, just as they did on the king. The hall would not only be large and tall, but would have the largest window, designed to light the dining table and to show to the outside world that this was an important room. Similarly this was the principal part of the house to be decorated. It might be spanned by an ornate timber frame, and have a certain amount of carving, for instance around doorways, even when the rest of the house was left plain.

The fire in many halls served the needs of cooking and so provided more than just warmth and a symbol of hospitality. Nevertheless, since there was always an element of formality in the hall, it was necessary to have a service room where food was stored and prepared for cooking, and where all the kitchen utensils could be kept out of the way. This all-purpose service room was usually partitioned from the hall so as to be conveniently close to the cooking hearth, and sometimes it was itself partitioned to make two separate rooms. They went by a number of names, such as pantry (or breadroom), buttery (or bottlery), milk-house or brewhouse.

From the start, kings had a private room known as a bower where they would retire to sleep. At first these were structurally separate from the hall, but they came to be included in the main building, again by being partitioned from the hall. What was a necessity for kings descended down the social ladder to manorial lords, eventually to reach the peasantry. So it came about that, by the later fourteenth century, Chaucer could describe even the poor widow of the 'Nun's Priest's Tale' in his *Canterbury Tales* as living in a cottage, with a hall and bower made sooty by the smoke of an open fire.

By this time the Old English word bower was giving way to the fashionable French word chamber, especially in the more advanced south of England. In the north a bower remained a bower until the end of the Middle Ages, and the hall, in a characteristically down-to-earth way, was usually called the firehouse, the house-body or house-part, or even simply the house; and this continued until well into the eighteenth century, such was this room's continuing pre-eminence in the smaller houses of the region.

The bower or chamber of a peasant's house was where the head of the house and his wife slept, but it might contain other beds for the rest of the household. Chaucer made a hilarious bedroom farce out of this in his tale of the miller of Trumpington. Invariably the chamber had to double as a store room. Sometimes it was built in a loft or in a full upper storey over the service room, but in the grander houses of medieval yeomen, the service room and the chamber were built, both at ground level, at opposite ends of the hall.

These became known as the lower and upper ends of the hall, since the upper end was where the lord's table was placed, often on a dais, to keep it from the dirt of an

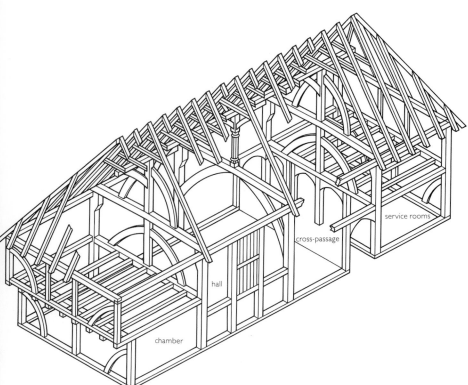

A cut-away perspective drawing of a three-part hall-house, showing the open hall in the centre, flanked by a chamber bay to the left and a service bay to the right. Smoke from a fire in the centre of the hall would find its way out through the roof, blackening the roof rafters in the process, and leaving a clue to the origin of the house that often outlasts other more obvious ones. The ground-floor chamber on the left served as the principal retiring and sleeping room, the floored room over it was used for storage and perhaps as a bedroom.

Beyond the cross-passage linking the front and back entrances to the hall are a pair of arched doorways leading into two service rooms. One of these might be called a brewhouse or milk-house, perhaps even a buttery (from the French *bouteillerie*, meaning bottle store); and the other a pantry (from the French *pain* for bread).

The floored room above might be for sleeping, but would certainly also be a store, for grain, or other agricultural produce.

earthen floor. In the houses of even the richer yeomen there was usually no dais, but the idea of a high formal end, the lord's domain, close to his chamber, and a low servants' end, close to the service room, remained valid and affected the peasantry, even though master and servant lived cheek by jowl. This was not the least because the low end was also where the entrance to the hall was placed and it was consequently less private.

The chamber at the high end was nevertheless usually a ground-floor room, for in the countryside people preferred to sleep downstairs, even when both the chamber and the service room had floors for lofts or full-height rooms built over them. These upper rooms might be used as sleeping rooms, but usually by the rest of the household and perhaps by guests, not the master and his wife.

The household consisted equally of younger members of the family and the servants. Servants were usually teenagers drawn from other families who stayed until their twenties, when, if they were lucky, they came into an inheritance or married and set up a home of their own to become a housebondman (husband) and housewife. The servants were treated as almost equal members of what in essence was at once a social and an economic unit which had to work together with little division except for a recognition of the authority of the master. A member of an older generation might occupy a chamber specially set aside, perhaps as a condition of a will; but short life expectancy and late marriage restricted the likelihood of more than two generations occupying a house together for long.

Because the household had an economic role, the house had to serve as a unit of production as well as a home. That meant that the upper rooms were always used for stores. They might be filled with grain, which had to be stored in a secure room where it could be kept dry and away from vermin, and other uses for these rooms were as cheese lofts, apple stores and dumps for all the tools and materials of cottage industry such as looms and bales of yarn.

The resulting linear plan of three rooms in a row — chamber, hall and service room — was a necessity because houses were built up from a number of standard timber trusses forming bays. The chamber could be built over the service room in a single bay, but often each occupied a separate bay, and there would be one or two more for the hall. This greatly eased construction, not least in the provision of an efficient pitched roof, and it satisfied a further need: both the front and back of the hall consequently remained free of building, so that its windows, which in the Middle Ages were still usually unglazed, could provide light on opposite sides. This was particularly necessary in bad weather as shutters could be closed on the windward side, leaving the windows open on the leeward side to provide adequate lighting.

Houses with this ubiquitous form were known even in the late Middle Ages as halls or hall-houses, although they might be the homes of comparatively poor peasants. Because so many of these hall-houses were substantially built, as thousands were in the villages of Kent alone, and many more thousands were in the rest of the country, they can still be found in great numbers today, although most of them have been greatly adapted to bring them up to modern standards.

Even when a medieval hall has been altered by inserting an enclosed hearth and chimney-stack and a new floor to form a continuous upper storey, it is often possible to visualize its original appearance. It is a lot harder to achieve it in practice. Too much space and convenience have to be sacrificed, and, for that matter, too much ancient craftsmanship has to be swept away as well.

These two perspectives show a much altered hall in Bedfordshire (A) as it might have been when new, and a hall in Norfolk (B), as it has been restored, with as good a compromise between the needs of today and the desire to have so large a space at the centre of the house. Even so, there is no open fire here, and a modern extension at the rear of the house makes up for the lost accommodation in the upper part of the hall.

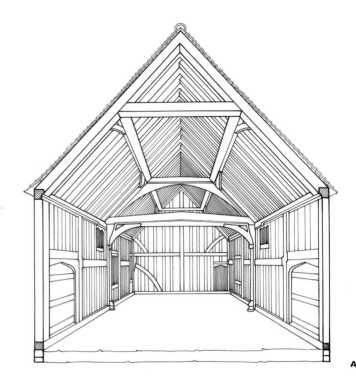

A

B

Kent has the greatest concentration of large medieval houses in the United Kingdom, and probably in all Europe. This farmhouse at Langley (C) is a good example of the original appearance of such houses, even to retaining its large hall window, albeit now glazed, and only the chimney-stacks are completely alien to the original design. The recessed centre and the overall roof are typical of the county, and of Sussex as well; in these two counties they can be seen in hundreds of surviving houses built between about 1370 and 1530.

C

The plan of a rural three-part hall-house (D) is instantly recognizable, with its open hall here occupying two bays of the timber frame, flanked by a chamber (LEFT), and two service rooms (RIGHT) beyond the front and rear entrances. Houses like this can be found all over England, except for the north, and in eastern counties of Wales.

In towns it was different, and compromises had to be made to fit hall, chamber and services into a long plot with narrow frontage. Access and lighting were the main problems. Here, in a much altered hall-house in Exeter (E), which has now been demolished, a side passage led past a shop, perhaps with a chamber over it, beside the open hall, to a courtyard at the rear and, beyond it, to a separate kitchen to minimize the risk of fire. Typical of the West Country, the design employed stone for the party walls, and the rest was built of timber. In a few parts of the country stone was readily available and merchants were rich enough to afford it, but mostly it was too expensive. The only recourse then was to timber, so plans of houses in towns differed fairly widely.

E

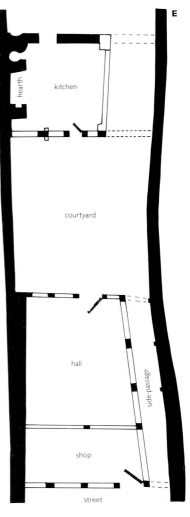

hearth

kitchen

courtyard

hall

side-passage

shop

street

D

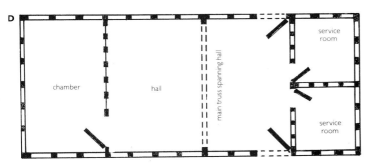

chamber

hall

main truss spanning hall

service room

service room

Views of two regularly laid-out terrace of timber-framed houses. Lady Row at York (A) was built in about 1316 with one room up and one room down. Church Street, Tewkesbury (B) was built over a century later with the addition of an open hall at the rear, and now well restored to show the original layout of the houses.

A

B

A perspective drawing of the restored interior of one of the Church Street. Tewkesbury (c). houses, which is now a museum. At the front is a shop, which could double for the manufacture and sale of goods, with a chamber over it for storing goods as well as for sleeping; then comes the open hall at the rear. So little accommodation did not suffice for long, and so a service room was added to the rear of many houses. This greatly restricted the light in the hall to what percolated through from the front and from the new back room.

C

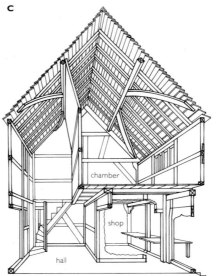

Urban hall-houses

Hall-houses were also built in towns, and in rich towns like Southampton, Bristol, Norwich, York and, above all, London there must again have been thousands of them. In towns the pressure to redevelop has always been greater than in the countryside, and the effects of fire, of bombing in the Second World War, and, ironically, of planning afterwards have been equally devastating. Consequently far fewer urban hall-houses survive, and are generally in a far more altered condition.

In towns the pressure on space is acute, and frontage on to a road is even more precious. The expansive plan of a rural hall-house with its hall flanked by a chamber and service rooms could only be used by the rich, and most builders had to contract the plan, or turn it sideways to run backwards from the street. All this meant accepting various modifications simply to ensure that rooms received enough daylight and that their construction did not become hopelessly complicated.

That was the aim, but in most prosperous towns business expanded and eventually the number of houses grew to match it. As a result, the pressure on land could mount so far that it led to so-called rookeries, where a house became lost within countless additions and accretions that piled room upon room around it. This disastrous mass of building heaped contagion and conflagration on its inhabitants. Indeed, parts of some towns developed a reputation so odorous that people shunned them like the plague.

One way to bring order to the threatening chaos of town building was to build to a regular plan. This was achieved in a number of towns, and never more successfully than when a single landlord could oversee the building of a uniform terrace of houses. This was happening in London at least by the start of the fourteenth century. The physical evidence of the houses themselves has long since been destroyed, but it survives in York. Here in 1316 the Vicar of Holy Trinity Church apparently built a regular terrace of houses, known as Lady Row, on the edge of the churchyard fronting Goodramgate, and seven of them can still be seen. Then there is Vicar's Close at Wells, a spectacular street built later in the century on the north side of the cathedral, and lined on each side with what were once uniform terrace houses. Possibly the finest medieval terrace of all lies in Church Street, Tewkesbury, just to the north of the abbey. Thanks to their skilful restoration, the full impact of this long row of identical timber-framed houses clearly shows that a terrace is meant to be more than the sum of its parts. Moreover, one of the houses has been restored as a museum, so it is possible to understand exactly what it meant to occupy a vertical slice of a medieval terrace.

At the front of each of these houses, a chamber or bower was built over a shop where goods could be both manufactured and sold, and behind these was an open hall. That was better than the one room up and one room down of Lady Row, but the houses in Tewkesbury were later extended rearwards beyond the hall to make a fourth room, although this meant removing the back windows from the hall and most of its light. The evident difficulty of fitting enough accommodation into the narrow plot occupied by each house was to be a recurrent problem in most town houses, and so was the difficulty of lighting them, especially at the rear where succeeding generations always wanted to build on extra rooms in extensions.

There is a much altered terrace at Battle in Sussex, and a few other once-ordered terraces of this kind survive in other towns. To build a terrace a single-minded landlord was needed who would risk his capital in building a number of comparatively expensive houses, in the hopes of leasing them to occupiers willing to pay top prices for the superior accommodation they offered. The Church was in this position in the Middle Ages, and it seems to have been responsible for many surviving medieval terraces. There were few strong incentives to do this while towns remained small, so most surviving medieval town houses were built individually and, at most, only loosely followed the layout and shape of their neighbours.

In the sixteenth and seventeenth centuries there were great changes in house building. These resulted from a large class of merchants and yeomen becoming able to afford the cost of brick and stone. By the end of the seventeenth century a house could generally be built entirely of these materials more cheaply than of timber. On top of that, glass also became cheaper and so it came into widespread use too. These changes first affected how people lived by making them want their fires to be enclosed within brick or stone chimney-stacks. Although these made fires burn more quickly and concentrated the heat in an unpleasant fashion, it was only conservative people who minded. Enclosed fires were perhaps safer and certainly cleaner, so the open hearth dropped out of fashion, taking the hall with it. While the word hall remained for a long time, an upper floor was now inserted into it – another advantage – and new houses with continuous upper floors from end to end became common. As for all the open hall-houses in Kent and elsewhere in the country, it was a relatively simple matter to build a chimney-stack against one of the walls in the hall and then throw a floor across the hall, so dividing the space into a ground and an upper storey.

This process took well over two centuries to achieve. While merchants and yeomen had built themselves the first fully storeyed houses with brick chimney-stacks by 1500, others were still building old-fashioned open halls in the south-east thirty years later, and in the Midlands and north this went on much longer. Medieval halls took longer to convert, and even in rich Kent some of them still remained unmodernized by the time of Celia Fiennes's journey in 1697. Again, in the north some open halls, or firehouses as they were called, remained open to the roof until well into the nineteenth century.

The first consequences of building chimney-stacks were slight, beyond the provision of an upper storey from end to end of a house. The new upper floor was still mainly used for storage or for bedrooms for children and servants. The old three-part arrangement of downstairs rooms still survived with the head of the house sleeping in the chamber, now increasingly called a parlour. This still lay at one end of the hall, now divided into two storeys, and the room at the further end was still used for storing and preparing food. There were various possible positions for the single chimney-stack, all of which had various advantages and disadvantages in terms of

Early houses with chimney-stacks differed little in their arrangement from the hall-houses they succeeded. This farmhouse at Fordham, Essex, seems to have been built by someone who had no idea how far an enclosed hearth could revolutionize the plan of a house. The chimney-stack was conceived as little more than an addition, as was the upper floor it made possible. Nevertheless, they are original features, although the front porch was in fact an addition made in 1583, a good half century after the house had been first completed. The brick section beyond it is later still.

Practically no hall-houses were left with their original open hearths, though the process of converting them took at least two centuries, even in a county as rich as Kent. This enclosed hearth and its attendant chimney-stack were probably inserted into the hall of a house at Cuxton, Kent, in about 1600, that is at least a hundred years after the house was built. Other houses in Kent had to wait a further hundred years before they were brought up to the same standard. In the north the process took much longer still.

planning and convenience. For the sake of cooking, it was best placed near the service room, but then it could not provide much heat in the chamber. If it was placed near the chamber, the food had to pass the dining table in the hall on its way from the service room to the fire where it was cooked. It was all very confusing.

Regional developments

For the whole of the sixteenth century and at least the first half of the seventeenth century, a great variety of house plans was tried, many of them evolved from the hall-house, others attempting to marry a brick chimney-stack and a timber frame in a more rational way that allowed the stack to provide back-to-back hearths on each floor and still leave room for a well-placed entrance and a staircase. These houses fell into regional types which can be further distinguished by the local materials from which they are made. Altogether their various characters are so strongly marked that the term vernacular architecture has been coined to describe them and the farm buildings that so often accompany them.

Eventually house builders became aware that hearths and chimney-stacks could easily be built into brick or stone walls. They realized that windows filled with glass kept out the weather whatever the wind, so that rooms did not need to have windows and consequently outside walls on both sides. Then a house could be built compactly with four rooms on each floor, filling a roughly square plan. Such houses were called 'double piles' because they had one range of usually two rooms at the front and another range of two at the back, built as though they were two piles placed together. As often as not the rooms were divided by a central entrance vestibule which led from the front door between the rooms to a staircase and a back door. Here was a standard plan that might have been used more often than it was if people had been both less conservative and less ignorant of up-to-date ideas, and if the countryside did not already possess so large a stock of houses for its farmers.

While it was difficult to make a roof cover a house as deep as a double pile without awkward, possibly leaky gutters, the plan had several clear advantages. It used a smaller quantity of building materials than a comparable house built with its rooms in a line, and this change in planning also made it both convenient and commodious. Its four-square shape was also an excellent vehicle for the new classical taste.

The four ground-floor rooms of the double pile were used in various ways. Generally the front rooms were for formal or family use. They might serve as a withdrawing room and a dining room, but in a farmhouse, they took on the more traditional roles of a private room or parlour and a public room or hall. The back rooms were usually for the servants, and comprised a kitchen and one or more service rooms. Sometimes one of these back rooms might be a living room for servants and an eating room for farm labourers as well. The rooms upstairs were used as bedrooms, even by the master in the eighteenth century, and sleeping downstairs became a thing of the past except among the poor.

This division between front and back was an architectural expression of widening social divisions between master and servant. While double piles had been widely built in medieval towns because they were economical in land, they were only accepted on a large scale in the countryside in the later seventeenth century, that is just as class divisions began to matter enough for the household of family and servants no longer to wish to live together in the old way.

This coincided with the time when the full implications of the discovery of the Italian Renaissance style at the hands of the architect Inigo Jones were at last affecting builders. Slowly the new style transformed the appearance of their houses all over the country. By the time of the Restoration in 1660, the old forms which had continued throughout the Tudor period into the seventeenth century were beginning to look rather dated to all but the most rustic and the most northern eyes. The most visible consequence was that the new houses no longer clearly belonged to a local pattern of building, and only the local materials from which they were made distinguished their origins.

The double pile and the classical style in which it could so easily be dressed became the norm for rural houses until well into the nineteenth century. Only the Victorians' pleasure in the picturesque and a desire to revive the styles of their yeoman ancestors, in what came to be known as the Old English or Vernacular Revival style, led to the double pile bowing to less regular though hardly more convenient forms.

This farmhouse at Long Whatton, Leicestershire, was built as a double pile about 1700. The difficulty in roofing so great a span was turned to advantage here with an array of gables along the front, even though they were increasingly falling out of favour in the more style-conscious south.

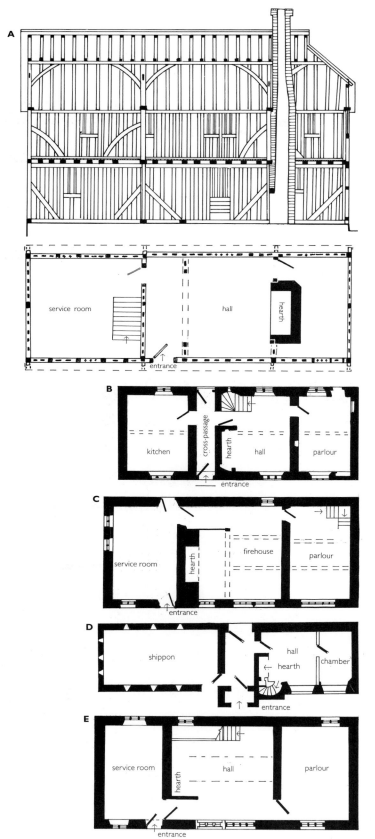

Plans

During the sixteenth century and the early years of the seventeenth, house builders devised a great variety of plans to take advantage of the freedom that an enclosed hearth and chimney-stack allowed. Many were guided by local tradition, and even the appearance of cheap glass did not immediately cause builders to abandon the long-established linear arrangement of rooms.

Floored halls

A common plan in the south-east (A) was in essence the three-part hall-house plan with a chimney-stack inserted at the end of the hall further from the entrance. This was good for warmth, but the food had to travel a long way between the service rooms where it was prepared and the fireplace in the hall where it was cooked; worse, it had to pass the table in the hall, and this was confusing. Nevertheless, as the section above the plan shows, the stack did allow a continuous floor to run from end to end, so making the upper part much more useful.

In stone houses (B) the hearth was often placed to back the cross-passage and in this way it helped to form one of its walls. The disadvantage of this arrangement was that the stack could not have a second hearth in its back, as a fire would be of little use in the passage, but further stacks could eventually be formed in the end walls to serve the other rooms without too much expense. In the north (c) this plan was greatly favoured, although, despite the harsher weather in winter, the entrances sometimes opened directly into the service room, or downhouse.

Long-house

In both the West Country (D) and the north, the service room was often used to stall cattle. Depending on the locality, this was called a shippon, mistal or byre and together with the living room formed what is now known as a long-house. Few long-houses remain in their original double use today.

In the north, the entrance continued to open directly into the hall (E) or into the service room (F), though a wooden screen known as a heck sheltered the hearth and the ingle in which the fire burned from the worst draughts coming from the doorway.

Lobby entry

Where timber-framing remained the commonest method of building, a new plan was devised in the first quarter of the sixteenth century whereby the entrance opened not into a passage, but into a small lobby with the chimney-stack behind it (G); these were set within a narrow bay of framing for mutual support and the bay usually contained the staircase as well.

The rooms on both sides had a hearth; on one side was a parlour, the new word for a chamber, on the other a hall-kitchen with a larger fireplace for cooking. It took at least half a century before this new plan became popular, even though the arrangement allowed both of the rooms upstairs to have fireplaces of their own. By the eighteenth century the rooms upstairs were being used as bedrooms in the modern fashion.

This so-called lobby-entry plan was very convenient until more than two rooms were wanted per storey. Indeed, the plan was so popular that it was soon used for stone and brick houses as well (H), even though this was an inefficient use of space and materials since, when the walls were solidly built of stone or brick, the stacks could be better placed on the external walls.

A parallel development in the stone houses of the north led to two-roomed houses being built in the seventeenth and eighteenth centuries with a chimney-stack in a gable wall and an entrance and shielding heck beside it (I), but these houses lacked a heated room at their other end.

The obvious solution for the increasing numbers of brick and stone houses being built in the seventeenth century was to incorporate chimney-stacks in the end walls (J); then a central

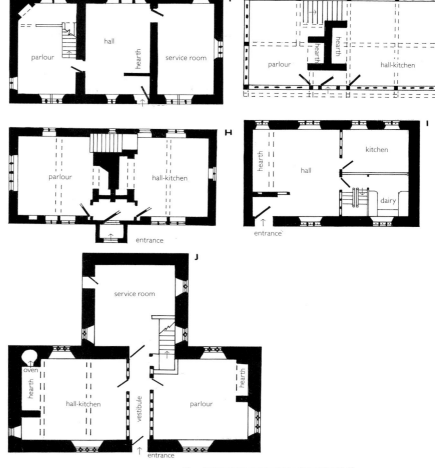

vestibule could provide access to rooms on each side, to a staircase to the upper floors, and perhaps to a small rear extension for a service room or dairy on the cooler north side of the house.

Double pile

Glazing and the freedom to plan for rooms having windows on only one side led to the adoption of the double-pile plan (K). Many arrangements of staircase and chimney-stacks were possible, but always the wide span of the roof was a problem. A central vestibule made access easy as well as giving the rooms complete privacy, but in the north the old idea of an entrance directly into the firehouse remained throughout the seventeenth century and well into the eighteenth (L).

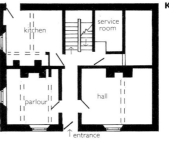

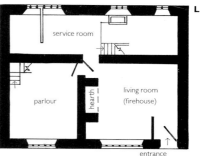

Terrace housing

The double pile fell out of use when it came to building in towns, except for the large houses of aristocrats, merchants and professional men so rich that they could afford a double-fronted plot. The norm was a narrow plot between about 15 and 25 feet wide, though it might extend ten times as far to the rear. The best way to build a house that was both cheap and commodious lay in the terrace, though the penalty was to build upwards with all the inconvenience of a fresh staircase linking each floor and the pair of rooms it contained. A double-pile house could easily provide eight rooms with only one staircase of, say, fifteen steps to link them; a terrace house with eight rooms had to be built on four floors and consequently needed three times as many staircases and steps.

Perhaps there is something essentially English and democratic, or at least egalitarian, about this solution, since every household had a vertical share of the terrace, unlike in France, where apartments all on one floor became the norm, and some had to climb further than others to reach them. Nevertheless democracy has its limits, and the English – and the Americans too, for they adopted the terrace or 'row' – allowed the servants to live at the top of the house and work in the basement, so they had the most climbing to do. The social division in the double pile between front and back became a division between upstairs and downstairs in the terrace.

It is not clear how the standard terrace house of the eighteenth century developed with all its floors from the medieval terrace house with its open hall. One stage of development was to adapt construction from timber to brick or stone. This had several implications; one was that the chimney-stack would be most economically placed against the party wall dividing one house from its neighbour. Nevertheless one short terrace of four houses in Islington was built of brick in 1658 with the chimney-stacks rising through the centre of each house as though it were still built of timber. The standard plan had not yet been developed, nor had it even in the 1680s when terrace houses were commonly built with their chimney-stacks built into the party wall, but with their staircases set against the party wall between the front and back rooms in an inconvenient way that seems to derive from rural practice. The trouble with this arrangement was that it left the staircase without any other natural lighting than could be provided by either a wasteful light well or a leak-prone lantern set in the roof.

By 1700 or soon after, the standard terrace house plan had evolved. So successful was it that it has never needed much further alteration. From the front door at one side of the front of the house a passage runs along one party wall to the stairs at the back, which are lit by windows on the rear wall. The passage gives access to a room at the front and another at the back, which have their fireplaces on the further party wall. The stairs lead down to a basement and up to one or more further floors, all with two main rooms each. How the rooms were used was up to the occupants, though generally the basement contained a kitchen and service room where the servants worked and might even sleep. If the basement had an open area before it, the servants and tradesmen would have their own entrance here, and a cellar could be

The elegance of the terrace has always captivated town dwellers, yet it rests on a few, simple elements – windows and doors – and a little decoration – stucco mouldings and cast-iron railings – harmoniously balancing each other. Spoil just one of them and the overall effect is completely ruined.

built out under the pavement for coal and stores. The ground and first floors were the most important and contained reception rooms, but they could also contain parlours and bedrooms. The top floors again could contain bedrooms, nurseries and servants' rooms, depending on the individual needs of the household. The great convenience was that all rooms could have fair-sized windows facing either front or back, and every room could have its own fireplace.

So far as lighting was concerned, not only did every room have at least one window and the staircase one per flight, but even the passage from the front door could receive enough light from a window placed over the door. This was often in the semicircular shape of a fan, but it came to be known as a fanlight regardless of its shape. Other conveniences included large cupboards or very small rooms known euphemistically as closets, and sometimes as necessary rooms; here chamber pots were kept before and after use because sanitation was so much more difficult a problem in towns than in the countryside. Behind the house in a yard or a garden there might be a cess pit, and the house depended on the scavengers who took all kinds of household waste out to the market gardens on the fringes of town as manure. Running water was largely absent until the nineteenth century, and houses had to rely on public supplies if they did not have a pump of their own, either in the basement or out in the backyard.

In this form, the terrace successfully solved the old problems of heating, lighting and circulation within the narrow confines of crowded towns, and provided a fair degree of privacy at the same time. It did this with style and economy, qualities that suited both the speculators who invested their money to run up these houses by the hundred in every expanding town in the land, and the aspirations of occupants who wanted a fashionable house and a good address.

As an insurance against the risks of fire and collapse, a number of laws were passed that attempted to regulate house construction. There had been laws to control building with the aim of reducing the consequences of fire in the Middle Ages, and more followed the Great Fire of London, starting with the Act for the Rebuilding of the City of London of 1667. Only the 1774 Building Act gave London really effective laws to outlaw jerry-builders as well as to reduce the risk of fire spreading from one house to another, and other towns had to await the later nineteenth century and the passing of local by-laws to achieve the same ends.

There was one problem that these laws did not at first solve, and this remained endemic in crowded towns until pure running water and hygienic mains drainage came to the rescue. With its closets and maybe a cess pit or an open sewer on the one hand and a poor water supply from pipes that at best brought water from close to where sewage was discharged, health remained nearly as much at risk in these houses as in others built with less attention to planning and style. London solved its problems by building a new sewerage system in 1865, but similar progress was very slow in many towns and reformers had to fight for the adoption of by-laws—and, of course, their enforcement—to achieve significant improvements in standards of public health.

A fanlight, complete with the radiating glazing pattern that gave it its name, here accentuated by the radiating brick and Coade stone voussoirs of the arch and the keystone, typically bearing a decorative mask (RIGHT).

As a remarkable solution to a difficult problem, the terrace continues to serve more than fashion. In towns, where frontage was limited, the ordered terrace (BELOW) was favoured more and more as the seventeenth century progressed. After the Great Fire of London, it was blessed by Act of Parliament. Space, building materials and profits could all be maximized, and the terrace house attained a degree of status that it has never entirely lost. It was highly convenient, offering the greatest flexibility and only one drawback – the stairs. The three flights between basement and attic might mean forty or fifty individual steps.

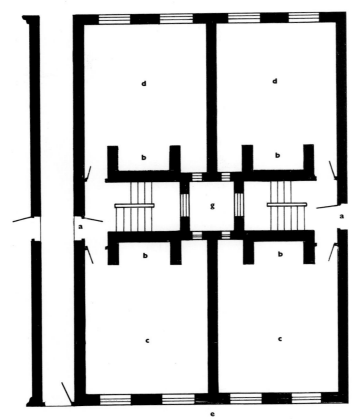

Only at the end of the seventeenth century did the terrace reach its standard form, with two rooms per storey, one at the front, one at the back. Earlier terraces (LEFT) had their chimney-stacks set within their party walls in an inefficient and space-wasting position, and their staircases were in the middle where they were difficult to light properly. With the chimney-stacks set against one party wall, and an entrance passage leading to a staircase set against the other (BELOW), all the major problems in the plan were resolved. There has been little need to modify it ever since.

Key

a entrance
b hearth
c front room
d back room
e street
f closet
g light well

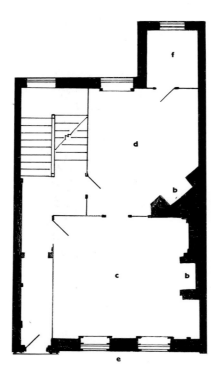

Slowly the proportions of the Georgian style faded during the early years of Queen Victoria's reign, and symmetry gave way to more picturesque effects and even old-fashioned details such as casement windows were revived. All these changes can be seen in this grand farmhouse at Kempton in Shropshire (BELOW). Because of its remote site, it still relies on local stone, an unusual bluish shalestone, but the bricks for the chimney-stacks and the Welsh slates on the roof have made long journeys to reach here.

The vigorous lines of the late Victorian Gothic house slowly gave way to a more welcoming, homely style based on the domestic architecture of the seventeenth and early eighteenth centuries. Not very accurately, it was called the 'Queen Anne' style. One of its first exponents was the architect Norman Shaw, whose grand Swan House on Chelsea Embankment, shown here, was built in 1875 (RIGHT). Its three bow windows were inspired by a seventeenth-century house in Ipswich, and its red bricks and prominent dormer windows could be widely found in houses of that period. The tall windows above the jetty of the second floor are quite original.

The mass-produced late Victorian terrace house is one of the commonest features of all towns where there was any building between 1880 and the Great War. It is found in all kinds of suburbs, such as here in Hither Green in south London, where an important railway goods yard brought new employment as well as a means of reaching old employment in inner London.

The vigorous outline of projecting bays and recessed porches, the multicoloured bricks and moulded stucco shown here are ubiquitous. The vaguely Gothic styling was a speculative builder's version of the style so fervently publicized to his eventual regret by the great Victorian critic and writer, John Ruskin. Nevertheless, these houses are soundly built and planned, and their detailing fits well into the places that most need it, notably in the arches over the porches and as capitals for the shafts which support the projecting bay windows.

Victorian innovations

It was only in the late nineteenth century, and then after appalling outbreaks of filthy diseases such as cholera and typhus, that public attention to health prompted action among the newly reformed local authorities to ensure supplies of pure water and adequate drainage. This slowly had its effect on house design. The terrace sprouted an enlarged back extension that once had housed no more than closets, now to receive the full benefits of the new amenities. Its ground floor included a scullery with piped running water feeding a sink. This had a properly trapped drain that would not allow bacterial emissions to enter the house from the newly laid sewers. A boiler in the scullery or the main kitchen provided hot water that again was piped to the sink. In the storey above the scullery there could be a bathroom, again with hot and cold water piped to a hand-basin and a fixed bath that at last made washing a private matter of some luxury when compared with the old use of tubs, laboriously filled by servants or set up in smaller households with little privacy before the living-room fire. Furthermore, hot water could even be piped to a number of cast-iron radiators within the house to offer primitive central heating.

A good water supply and mains drainage at last made it feasible to include a flushing water-closet as well. At first water-closets were set up outside in the traditional way for the sake of health. They were usually placed near the scullery, but separated for the sake of hygiene by being outside beside the coal store. It was only a matter of time for the water-closet to be brought indoors, often taking its place in the upper storey of the back extension alongside the bathroom. These new amenities not only made life much pleasanter and healthier, but they also satisfied Victorian moral attitudes, which viewed bodily functions as so private as to be practically unmentionable.

However much it eased problems that only troubled the darker recesses of the Victorian mind, the back extension tended to obscure some of the rear windows and certainly made houses generally darker. But help was at hand: at practically the same time another new amenity brought by the Industrial Revolution came to the rescue of the terrace house. This was in the form of gas lighting, which allowed light to enter a house at the turn of a tap. No sooner was this becoming common than electricity arrived to supersede it, but the full effects of this were largely for the twentieth century to exploit.

The twentieth century has turned the house into a focus of consumption. This has, of course, had many benefits. In particular, standards of hygiene have been raised, making the house a healthier place for those who could afford such improvements. Sadly, many houses were condemned after the Second World War as sub-standard and were demolished rather than improved. New blocks of flats and maisonettes were built rapidly to take their place but they soon decayed because they were shoddily built and poorly maintained. Adapting the old housing stock would often have been a better course to take.

The history of the English house is therefore one of continuity and evolution. That makes it adaptable, whenever it was first built, and there is hardly an old house that

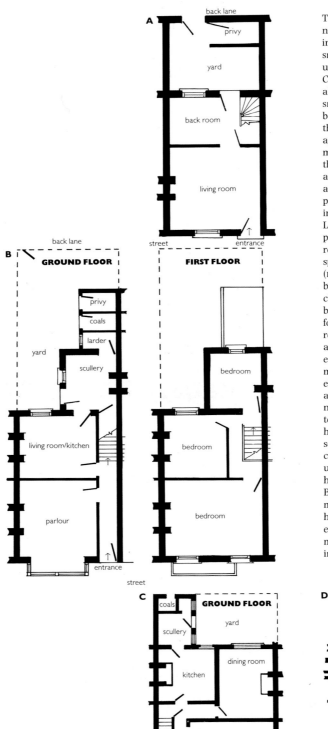

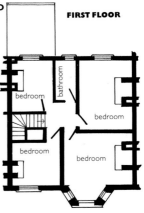

The terrace houses built for the new population of urban industrial workers were often very small and have given us the two-up two-down houses of Coronation Street (A). This plan allowed for a living room and a small scullery **below** two small bedrooms. In a poky backyard there would be a privy, an appalling health hazard. In the middle of the nineteenth century, the effects of urban overcrowding and resulting disease reached such a pitch that the government passed legislation with the aim of improving housing standards. Local authorities were required to pass by-laws to enforce the regulations. This led to more spacious and better built houses (B), preferably with three bedrooms so that male and female children could sleep apart, and better arrangements were made for removing sewerage and other refuse. It was the eventual adoption of modern services, especially running water and mains drainage, and gas and then electric lighting, that brought about the modern house (C). The new amenities were first restricted to an extension at the rear of the house, since, oddly, they were not seen as objects of esteem as chimney-stacks and continuous upper floors had been four hundred years beforehand. Because back extensions took too much light from the rest of the house, the new amenities were eventually brought within the main walls, and fully integrated into the design of the house.

The period house gives Britain its most abiding image and its most rewarding experience (LEFT). Clearly it is something to treasure. But it is not only the old houses of our picturesque villages and country towns that count, or the proud terrace houses built on eighteenth-century estates; the Victorian and Edwardian houses of our suburbs (BELOW) may be more common, but when they are complete with their decorated doorways, windows, fireplaces and staircases, they, too, have a rarity value of their own.

has not been adapted in a number of ways. The lives of the people who occupied it over the years have changed in many ways. Machines, not servants, do much of the work nowadays. Comfort is a well-developed priority, and few could stand life in an open hall with its central hearth and unglazed windows. That is not to say that some semblance of an open hall cannot be recreated. Nevertheless, to do so means removing not just the mere accretions of later years, but the evidence of centuries of use, and this usually has a greater value than some notion of historical exactitude.

In many ways the best maxim for dealing with an old house is to leave well alone. What needs repair must have repair. What exists as a fragment may be reinstated as a whole, but only if that does not interfere with some other period feature, and there is enough evidence to be reasonably sure of its original appearance. Wholesale restoration to some specific period in the past is another matter. It can only be justified on a few occasions. It is fine for museums, such as the Weald and Downland Open Air Museum at Singleton in West Sussex, the Avoncroft Museum of Buildings near Bromsgrove in Worcestershire, or the Welsh Folk Museum at St Fagan's, Cardiff. It is not, however, fine for daily life. This course of action will always involve interpretation and much guesswork, so it is invariably open to many qualifications. What is not open to qualification is that an old house, given care, is a wonderful place to live in, and a source of everlasting satisfaction.

A Victorian terrace already shorn of some of its original features — the windows of the middle house, the front railings of all of them — and a bit forlorn as a result; but these could be easily brought back to their original and greatly improve the houses as a result.

Medieval houses

The vast majority of the houses of England's medieval peasantry do not survive. Those that do were built for men at least a cut above the average who lived in the last two centuries of the Middle Ages. The yeomen of Kent were exceptionally wealthy and, while their grand houses were common enough to account for perhaps a good half of all the houses standing in the county at the end of the Middle Ages, most people elsewhere had to make do with far smaller houses, such as the few remaining medieval ones at Stoneleigh in Warwickshire, or houses that were so insubstantially built that they lasted only a generation or so.

The medieval houses of Stoneleigh are remarkable survivors, but they have been greatly altered and enlarged over the years, simply to keep them in use. Even the medieval houses of Kent are as much the creations of the following centuries as of the century of their birth, so much have they been changed by succeeding generations. Apart from the inserted chimney-stacks and upper floors thrown across their formerly open halls, these houses invariably have new glazed windows in place of the old openings. Often the material filling the gaps in the old timber frame has been renewed, and sometimes whole walls have been hung with tiles, if not entirely rebuilt in brick. All in all, these houses are now replete with innumerable alterations made to keep them up to date, and a hundred and one amenities provided for the comfort of the generations that followed their builders.

Only a few peasants built their houses of stone in the Middle Ages, and most of these were around Dartmoor, where granite moorstone lay on the surface of the ground ready for use. The only decoration that could be achieved with this hardest of all building stones was fine ashlar work, that is the cutting of the stone into the regular blocks which made up a flat-faced wall. Occasionally these blocks were of immense size and could weigh a ton or so. How a mason and his assistant lifted them into position is unclear, but the use of these huge stones in a farmhouse wall seems to have brought an element of status with it.

Outside Kent and the south-east, Essex and parts of East Anglia, where timber-framing flourished from the start of the thirteenth century, and outside Dartmoor and a few other parts of the West Country where stone was cheap, medieval peasants built their houses with such insubstantial walls that it was a matter of status as well as convenience and durability to replace them with stone or brick. In Stoneleigh and much of the Midlands there is little good building stone, so brick was used. In parts of Dorset, Somerset and Gloucestershire, the few remaining medieval houses were reclad with stone walls, and similar recladding was commonly undertaken in the north. Even so, there are still a few places where houses built of unbaked earth survive. They are still common in Devon and East Anglia, and a few such houses remain in Cumbria.

All these changes mean that the original features of medieval houses are apt to be fragmentary, and a house with a full range of medieval features is remarkably rare. Even those that have become museum pieces have undergone extensive restoration. Therefore any fragment of medieval origin is to be treasured for its rarity, even if it can be inconvenient at the same time.

Timber-framing

The surviving medieval features may be restricted to fragments of timber-framing. This is now well understood, and most timber buildings follow local traditions of practice that allow a notional reconstruction of their original appearance to be made. This can provide various clues to the date when the frame was erected. Furthermore, by studying the differential rate of growth of the timber as shown in the rings of wood laid down each year – the study is called dendrochronology – the date when the timber was felled can sometimes be ascertained.

Timber-framing had two functions, structural and decorative. It provided the means of keeping a house upright indefinitely, and it brought status to the house and reflected esteem on the owner, just as a good address and a handsome house do today. The decorative elements of a timber frame may be the dour grandeur of closely spaced studs or the exuberant patterns formed by curved studs and braces. The type and variety of these patterns were greatly augmented immediately after the Middle Ages, notably in the later sixteenth century, but it was in the Middle Ages that they were first appreciated.

With luck an original timber doorway may survive; it may have a pointed arch and a chamfered or even a moulded surround reminiscent of the grander stone arches used for church doorways, and there could even be some form of carving around the head of the arch and an embattled parapet.

There is always the chance that fragments of medieval window frames may survive, especially near later, inserted glazed windows. The evidence may be no more than a series of diamond-shaped mortises cut into the underside of a wall-plate, showing where an open window was once protected by timber mullions. Occasionally the mullions themselves survive beneath a filling of daub which was applied to block the openings between them when modern windows were inserted elsewhere; more occasionally still, the heads of formerly open windows may retain the decorative Gothic tracery which once added status to the room they lit, usually the hall or a principal chamber.

Occasionally a post was carved with a capital, again usually with the form that could be found on the stone piers of a parish church. A favourite post to receive this carving was the corner post of a house, especially if it supported the diagonal or dragon beam which carried the joists of an overhanging or jettied upper floor. Inside the house, the frame spanning the two bays of an open hall was a favourite place for decoration, either in the form of curved braces or, again, in the form of carved capitals on the main posts.

The panels between the framing members were filled with wattles, often of springy hazel, bound together with pliable stems from various plants such as brambles; or the panels might be filled with interwoven laths. These were then covered with daub, a mixture made of clay, sand, lime and any earthy material available locally. This was strengthened with vegetable matter and cow hair. When dry, the mixture is remarkably strong and is a very good insulator, provided it does not crack and come away from the frame. It needs to be protected from the weather, and this was achieved by plastering and limewashing it regularly. When it was left too long the whole panel would have to be replaced. As a result, original medieval daub is fairly rare.

In many parts of the country both the plastered daub and the framing were limewashed and coloured. This was not with the exaggerated contrast of black and white that the Victorians so admired and applied to such excess in Cheshire above all other counties; instead, it was the earth colours, such as ochre and reddle (red ochre) and various vegetable dyes, which provided the warmly tinted yellows and reds, and occasionally greens and blues, that are still often seen on the timber houses of northern France. In England it is rare to find more than the slightest traces of original colouring in this form. Black and white have prevailed too widely, and, where they have not, a taste for oak bleached silver by sun and rain has killed off the tradition of colouring timber buildings. One thing medieval house-owners did not do was feed timber buildings with polish or other preservatives as though they were furniture, and there is no need to do it now. Modern wood preservatives, especially those that restrict the damage caused by insect attack, are a different matter, but there is no substitute for ensuring that no part of a frame is subject to continuous damp.

In northern Essex, adjacent parts of Hertfordshire, Cambridgeshire and Suffolk, and occasionally elsewhere, the whole timber frame was covered over or pargetted with a thick plaster coat. This could be combed or modelled before it had set into all kinds of incised or raised patterns. These were usually geometrical and confined to panels, though, especially after the Middle Ages, they came to include exotic patterns and figurative scenes. The trouble with patterned pargetting is that, if it becomes exposed, it does not last and so has to be reworked. To stop this happening, it needs to be regularly limewashed, but, like all forms of paint, the limewash builds up over the years until the originally crisp forms are smothered in a bumpy obscurity.

Roofs, doors and shutters

Medieval houses were usually thatched, if only because most peasants grew enough corn to provide the straw to cover their roofs. Thatch needed maintenance and had to be replaced every generation anyway. It admirably matched the impermanent nature of most medieval houses, but it was a poor partner for the roofs of houses with sound timber frames. By the thirteenth century, however, tiles were coming into use, thanks to a few specialized tile-making kilns operated by great builders such as the abbeys, so that, by the late fourteenth and fifteenth centuries, when large numbers of substantial peasant houses were at last being built in the south-east, it was common for wealthy yeomen to prefer tile to thatch on account of its greater durability and fire resistance. Elsewhere thatch remained common because it was cheaper, and in poor pastoral regions like the West Country and the north-west it was usual to resort to heather and other materials, because good wheat straw was unavailable and other forms of straw were too valuable as winter fodder for the animals.

Very occasionally a medieval house may still have its original door. Medieval doors were usually made from timber planks arranged vertically so that they would not retain rainwater, and battened and nailed together. More solid doors could have their planks tongued and grooved or be made from thicker studs into which planks were rebated, but these were uncommon in yeoman houses. Some doors were made of two layers of planks, an outer vertical layer with an inner layer set either horizontally or diagonally.

Door hinges seldom consisted of more than straps that terminated in rings which sat on iron pivots. Grand houses were given the ornate bracketed hinges and other iron door furniture such as the knobs and locks that are rare enough even in aristocratic houses and churches of the period. Catches might be no more than wooden or iron latches, and drawbars secured external doors.

The shutters which kept bad weather from penetrating a house through the larger windows were usually similar to doors, being simply battened planks hinged on iron pivots and kept in place by iron catches. The pivots were often substantial enough to survive, though the shutters were nearly always thrown out when the windows were glazed. The smallest windows were seldom shuttered, but intermediate windows often had horizontal shutters which slid across the windows in grooves cut into the sill and the plate above the windows. They too have only left the evidence of these grooves behind, and so have the rare shutters that were set in vertical runners to rise up from below the open window like the sashes of the Georgian period. Another way of reducing the effects of the weather was to fasten oiled linen across a window opening, and closely set pieces of straw also let in a little light and not all the weather. None of this survives today.

A few windows were not intended to provide light, only a flow of air. Such windows were a necessity for milk rooms and cheese lofts, which had to be kept cool and airy; they were consequently fitted with horizontal louvers to keep out the light. Probably none survive from the Middle Ages, but they remained in use until recently and several seventeenth-century farmhouses in the Severn Valley still retain louvered 'cheese windows' as evidence of their pastoral activities.

While the inside of a medieval house was more or less sheltered from exposure to the weather, it was less protected from the attentions of successive owners, and so the best chance for original features to survive came when the insertion of more fashionable ones hid them from sight. At once the most surprising and the most common is a decorative roof.

A hall gained much in status from carved posts and patterns made up from curved and cusped braces in its roof. When chimneys arrived and halls were divided by inserted floors, it was not very long before the new upper rooms were ceiled over, and the roof was forgotten. Though electricians rewiring a house or plumbers installing new central heating often report the soot on these roofs, mistaking it for the result of an accidental fire, they seldom see the decorative posts and braces in the darkness. It is very difficult to restore a roof like this to its original condition without either destroying the archaeological information provided by the layers of medieval soot, the exposed battens and the undersides of the roof tiles, or ruining the amenities of the roof space by removing its insulating properties and the pipes and wires and other services that it contains.

Only a wealthy yeoman could afford to have a hall highly decorated. Many halls were left without any decoration, other than in the roof. Two prized places for decoration were the door surrounds, particularly for the doors into the service rooms and into the chamber, and the beams at the upper end of the hall behind the high table. In a very grand yeoman hall there might be a cove, that is a form of canopy that curves upward and outward from the end wall, more to accentuate the importance of the high table than to cover it. It was made up from carved beams, top and bottom, and might be panelled and painted. More often there would simply be a single carved beam, perhaps with rich mouldings and an embattled parapet.

All the principal timbers in a grand house could have their edges chamfered, that is flattened, or have decorative mouldings cut into them, but it was after the Middle Ages that these really came into their own. As on the outside, the daubing between the timber members of the framing could once again be decorated with incised patterns, and the walls generally could be limewashed and coloured. Sometimes the walls were decorated with coloured geometrical or naturalistic patterns, and these, oddly, seem to have continued heedlessly over plaster and timber with no respect for the change in surface and level between them. The only other form of wall decoration was to hang up a painted cloth, a poor man's tapestry.

The ground floors of most medieval halls were made from earth. This was hardened by being mixed with clay and ox blood and beaten flat. In much of the chalkland of southern and eastern England floors were made of rammed chalk instead, and hardened with sour milk. Floors had no covering, but were strewn with straw or rushes. According to Erasmus the straw hid unspeakable filth – though he went so far as to mention refuse from the table, vomit and urine – and it is easy to see how rats flourished in medieval England and allowed the plague to spread so ferociously. Yet archaeologists have always been impressed by how well scoured medieval floors seem to have been, with the straw and other household rubbish regularly going out to the fields as manure.

Somewhere in the middle of the hall floor was the hearth. It was marked out by stones on which a wood fire would burn slowly on a heap of ash. A good fire gave out much heat but little smoke. In his *Piers Ploughman* Langland saw fit to curse anyone who let a fire smoke badly, so the assumption that medieval halls were always filthy and smoky should be treated with caution. Beside the fire were the irons that supported the pots and pans needed in cooking, but all of this, the earthen floor included, are now objects only for the archaeologist, since the requirements of public health have long since swept away or covered over the last remains of these primitive features from even the lowliest of poverty-stricken houses.

The upstairs floors were boarded, often with boards of around one foot wide, made from elm or chestnut as well as oak. Because they tended to warp, and gaps easily opened up between them as a house moved over the years, these old planks were often removed and replaced by narrower ones, and occasionally they were fossilized underneath when new planks were laid on top of them.

There is no escaping the fact that the medieval house is a thing of the past in a way that even sixteenth-century houses are not. Changed standards of living have left it behind. Nevertheless, its new-found permanence in the last centuries of the Middle Ages has left us with thousands of the better ones in a recognizable state. This is a unique legacy that should be respected. For the house of a peasant to survive five hundred years is a remarkable testament to its builders and first inhabitants alike. We owe its continuing survival to the future. That would be a small testament to us.

Forms of hall-house

Hall-houses come in a variety of forms, with the chamber and service ends expressed by jetties for instance, but not by separate gables in the roof, as in the Wealden house (A); or with one or both of the ends expressed by cross-wings with separate roofs; or not expressed outside in any way at all. Sometimes even the hall window was hardly larger than the others, as in this example from north-east Wales (B).

Most small peasant hall-houses did not have good enough framing to last long, and some had no framing at all. In some parts of the country, for instance East Devon (C), the walls were soundly made of cob. Such houses are often found in parts of the country where dairy farming flourished, and some of them were designed to have their service ends used for agricultural purposes, perhaps as cattle byres.

Even when they served as conventional service rooms, these houses were still small and the divisions between the central hall and the flanking chamber and services were only in the form of stud and plank partitions that hardly reached above head-height. People, and even their animals, lived cheek by jowl in a way that we cannot readily grasp today.

A

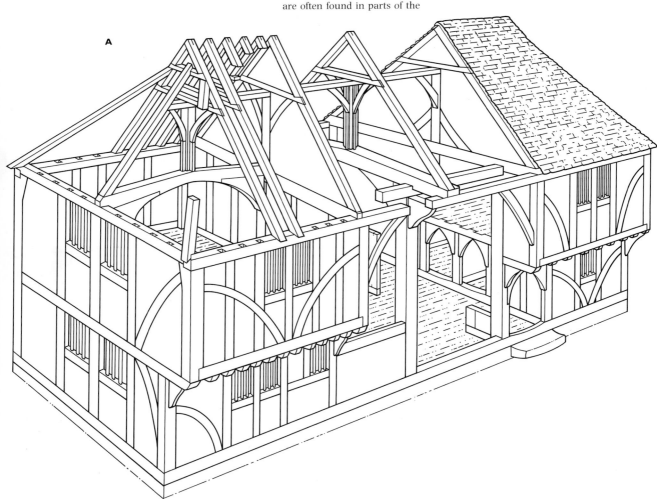

B

C

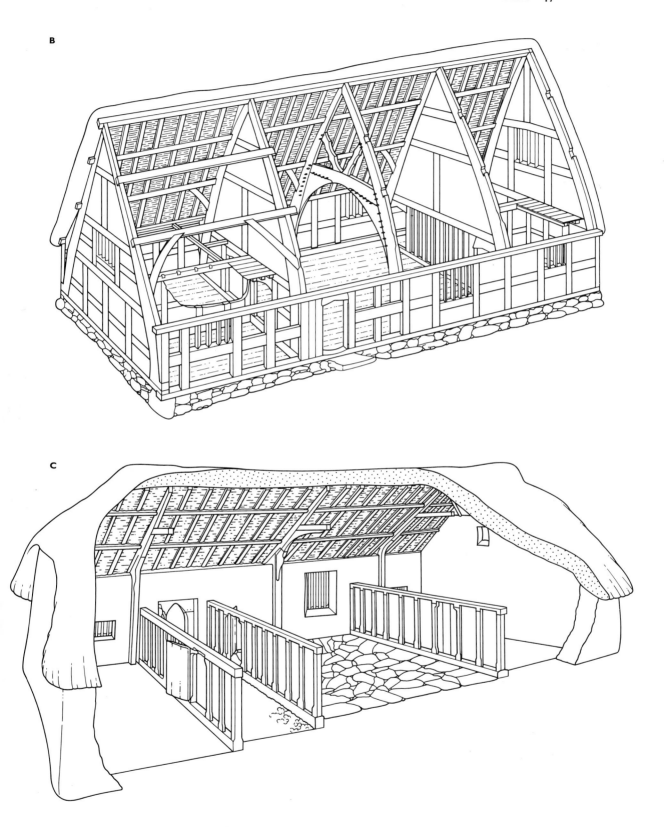

Two hall-houses

Kent's hall-houses are not the largest in the country, nor the most ornate, but nowhere else did English yeomen build so many of them in the last two hundred years of the Middle Ages; nor did they achieve so cohesive a design as in the so-called Wealden type of hall-house shown here at Langley, Kent (LEFT). The jetties at each end clearly mark the service rooms on the right beside the front door, and the chamber on the left, while the great overall, hipped roof integrates the three main parts into one architectural whole. The design is well balanced too, and only the entrance and the great hall window, here very well preserved, break the overall symmetry.

The smaller hall-house at Keysoe, Bedfordshire (RIGHT) is not immediately recognizable for what it is. It has been more altered, but still retains enough of its frame to make its original form clear when examined in detail. The house always had its chamber in a

separately roofed cross-wing and its service room in a continuation of the body of the house extending from the central hall. So neither the differentiation nor the integration of the Wealden design were ever evident here.

Small hall-houses

Most of the medieval peasantry's hall-houses have long since been demolished because they were too small or too poorly built to survive. This makes the village of Stoneleigh, south of Coventry, all the more remarkable for the number of small medieval hall-houses which still exist there in anything like a recognizable state. The house shown here (LEFT) has been modernized in a number of ways and now has walls solidly finished with brick nogging in the panels of its timber frame rather than its original flimsy wattle and daub infilling.

The Devon long-house on the edge of Dartmoor (BELOW) has hardly any more accommodation than the Stoneleigh house, since the right-hand end was built for a herd of cattle, not human occupation. For all that, there was one way in which this house

continued on page 53

The two facing rows of houses built in the middle of the fourteenth century to form the Vicars' Close at Wells, Somerset, are not just among the earliest surviving terraces but a remarkably regular example of medieval domestic planning. The front of a single house has been restored to show its medieval appearance. It has two rooms, a hall on the ground floor with a fireplace and chimney-stack built into the front wall, and a chamber above, reached by a newel stair on the rear wall. Many medieval houses in both town and country had more accommodation than this, but few of them were built in terraces. The vicars needed no more room, but they gained from the architectural status of occupying a house in this planned street.

When a house had a jetty on adjacent sides, a diagonal or dragon beam had to be inserted into the framing to carry the internal ends of the projecting joists. Where it projects at the corner, this beam is carried by a dragon post. These were made of massive timber and carved to give them even more emphasis. This carved dragon post at Bolton Percy near York (LEFT) continues the crenellated decoration beneath the cove on the right-hand wall. Above the masks, a series of cut mouldings of more usual type completes the capital.

The interior of the hall of Winkhurst from Boughbeech in Kent (BELOW), a small hall-house rebuilt at the Weald and Downland Open Air Museum at Singleton. It graphically demonstrates how little accommodation the smallest houses had in the Middle Ages, while other medieval houses rebuilt at the museum show that some rich yeomen did far better. Nevertheless this was a substantial, well-built house which was only threatened because its site was needed for a reservoir. The idea that such houses were filthy and smoky is not particularly apparent, although it must always have been draughty and cold in winter.

continued from page 50

went beyond nearly all other peasant houses in the country: it was built of stone. This was the granite moorstone that local farmers could take freely from Dartmoor, leaving them to find a means of carting it the short distance to their homesteads and, more expensively, the services of a mason to cut it and lay it for them. This made up for the lack of good building timber in this part of the country.

Outside Dartmoor, stone was too expensive and timber supplies were only a little better, so Devon yeomen had to make do with other materials. Unbaked earth, or cob, was widely used, as at this farmhouse at Christow (BELOW). The mixture of earth, clay, pebbles and a binding of organic material, such as brambles or straw, that goes by the name of cob in the West Country is surprisingly long-lasting, even in wet parts of the country, provided that damp is kept from penetrating the walls. That means a sound roof and a watertight base, which are sensible precautions for any house regardless of the materials used.

On the outside a good coating of plaster is all that is needed. It has wonderful thermal qualities, and keeps in the warmth in England's cold climate as well as it keeps out the heat in the deserts of New Mexico.

Many houses, formerly walled in cob or in poorer mud and stud, came to be rebuilt in stone when yeomen could at last afford it. This small hall-house at Chetnole in Dorset (BOTTOM) was probably built with stud walls, which were replaced by good local limestone in the sixteenth or seventeenth century. As a result they needed less maintenance, but stone does not make warm walls.

A

Key

a tie-beam
b wall-plate
c wall-post
d tenon in upper part of post
e recess for dovetail in underside of tie-beam
f housing for rafters
g underside of end of tie-beam
h dovetail
i mortise for tenoned end of post

B

C

D

E

Key

a wall-post
b wall-plate
c tie-beam, extended outwards to form jetty
d bressummer carried by jettied ends of tie-beam and floor joists (not shown)
e wall-post of upper storey, locking bressummer in position

Carpentry used in timber-framing

The development of carpentry in the twelfth and thirteenth centuries made it possible for buildings to last indefinitely if they were properly maintained and the timbers kept from persistent damp. This was because oak is fairly easy to cut when green, but soon dries to become iron hard, and only its sapwood harbours hole-boring insects.

Two separate traditions of framing a building developed. One relied on a box-frame which formed the side and end walls and directly supported the roof; the other relied on the support of independent, bowed A-frames known as cruck trusses, to which the walls and roof were attached.

Box-frames

The box-frame was both more widespread and more common, and, ultimately, more adaptable to advancing needs. Nevertheless, it needed very complicated carpentry to join its various timbers together strongly enough to make them capable of supporting a roof.

The most significant development in the carpentry of the box-frame was the stable method of joining a vertical post both to the horizontal plate which ran along the top of a wall, and to the horizontal tie-beam which crossed to the other side of the box and stopped the walls falling apart. Both horizontal timbers were under stress because they supported the roof. The plate carried the outward thrust of the feet of the rafters, and the tie-beam not only stopped the rafters from forcing the walls to splay outwards, but also carried much of the weight of the roof through various struts and posts.

The joint that enabled the three timbers to be efficiently connected to each other (A) was developed towards the end of the thirteenth century, and remained in use until the end of the eighteenth century. The post terminated in a pair of tenons, a low one which fitted into a mortise in the wall-plate, and a higher one in an extension of the post that ran up beside the plate to fit into a mortise in the underside of the tie-beam. The tie-beam, meanwhile, extended beyond this tenon to end in a dovetail joint which engaged in the top of the wall-plate and stopped it from moving outwards under the strain of the rafters.

Joints

Most buildings were too long to be framed by single lengths of timber, which seldom exceeded 20 or 25 feet, so a number of so-called scarf joints were devised to connect the longitudinal timbers. These had to be able to resist bending and twisting. The easiest joints were those used for sill-beams that rested on the ground or on a plinth (B) and consequently were supported underneath. Other timbers needed stronger joints. In the Middle Ages various joints were tried (C), always with the joint running across the timbers from side to side, sometimes on a splay, sometimes with mortises and tenons at the ends. In the sixteenth century, these joints gave way to others where the joint ran down the timbers from top to bottom instead (D).

A jetty required one of the most complicated series of joints (E), but, by separating the points where the various timbers joined each other, no single timber had to have so many mortises cut out of it that it became excessively weakened. This made the process of assembly easier. There was also the great advantage of allowing the floor-joists of the upper storey simply to rest on the wall-plate without any complicated joints.

At their inner ends (F), the floor joists were simply tenoned into a beam in a number of ways, while the outer end rested on a bressummer; to tenon them into beams at both ends would have made the assembly of a timber frame very much harder.

With jetties along adjacent sides of a building, an extra strong corner post called a dragon post (G) was needed to support a diagonal or dragon beam that carried the inner ends of the joists (H), seen here from inside and underneath.

Cruck trusses

The alternative tradition of framing made use of linked pairs of curved timbers known as crucks to form a highly stable, bulged A-frame that was independent of both walls and roof, but supported them without recourse to the complicated carpentry and erection procedure needed with the box-frame (I). Though crucks look more primitive and apparently were never used in the richest parts of the country, namely the south-east and East Anglia, there is no reason to suppose that they were developed earlier or were, at least at first, in any way inferior. At all events, a number of extremely grand halls were built using cruck frames in the West Midlands and adjacent parts of Wales.

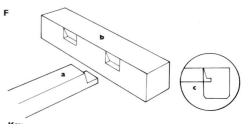

Key
a joist
b beam
c section through joint

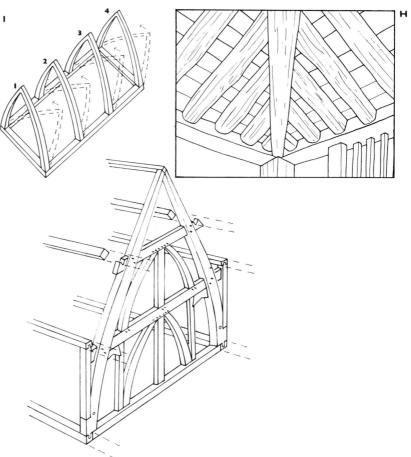

Details and decoration of timber-framed houses

A timber frame needed strengthening in a number of ways. One of the most important was to triangulate the corners with braces of various types. It soon became clear that these braces had all sorts of possibilities for decoration, and so in some houses there were far more braces than were strictly needed for stability: in others, the braces were hidden behind close-studding or panelling, in which timber was again used for display rather than strength.

Consequently a frame could be divided into main panels (A), to which curved braces could be added, rising to the wall-plate (B), or dropping down to a bressummer (C); occasionally both could be used across the corners (D), or from corner to corner (E), or in parallel curves (F). A rather more severe form of decoration was to divide the frame into small panels (G), or to fill it with closely spaced studs (H), and hide the braces behind them.

A late medieval house in Walmgate, York, combines curved braces in three different ways in a splendid demonstration of the carpenter's art (I). A roughly contemporary house at Pembridge, Herefordshire, has a frame divided into a series of panels (J), and no braces are visible at all.

Downward-curving braces are typical of Kent, but upward-curving braces were also needed to support the eaves of the roof where it bridged the recessed hall between the two jettied ends of a Wealden hall-house, such as this one at Cuxton (K). By the second half of the fifteenth century it was more fashionable in the south-east to hide all the bracing behind close-studding, as here in a magnificent yeoman hall-house at High Hurstwood, East Sussex (L). Square panelling was often used for the walls of cruck-framed houses, even though the panels were seemingly at odds with the curves of the crucks such as this one at Betley, Staffordshire (M). In the West Midlands, taste also turned to square panelling, as can be seen at an equally grand hall-house near Ledbury, Herefordshire (N).

Restoring timber frames

Because most timbers were mortised or halved together to build up a frame, they left behind mortise holes or trenches in the connecting timbers if they were removed. From this evidence it is often quite clear what has been removed and it is therefore possible to restore it quite accurately. Pieces of oak can readily be scarfed together, with rotten parts of an individual timber replaced in the same way. This is a form of restoration requiring great care using wet timber but it can produce better results than introducing steel beams, ties and bolts.

J

L

K

M

N

A

Entrances

The entrances of medieval houses were always important architecturally because they gave a visitor his first impression of a house. Few of them have survived, and usually in fragmentary form because the original doors have been replaced by new ones of a different size. This means that the doorway has also been altered in order to accommodate them.

Often the entrances were arched, as they were in grander buildings. This was usual if they were made of stone, although that was rare among yeoman houses. The arched entrance of a farm at Norton St Philip, Somerset (A), may result from its connection with Hinton Priory. The massive arch of the porch of a Dartmoor long-house (B) shows not only the huge individual stones used there, but also the typically shouldered shape of internal doorways found in late medieval houses in Devon. The flatter timber arch of the entrance at Cuxton, Kent (C), is

B

typical of late medieval doorways
in timber-framed houses.

A richer variation of the flat-
arched type of entrance had
carving in the spandrels or spaces
over the arch, and an embattled
parapet (D). By the late Middle
Ages, this allusion to the defensive
needs of the castles of an earlier
age had become simply a
decorative appeal to chivalry and
a forerunner of our current taste
for things of the past.

C

D

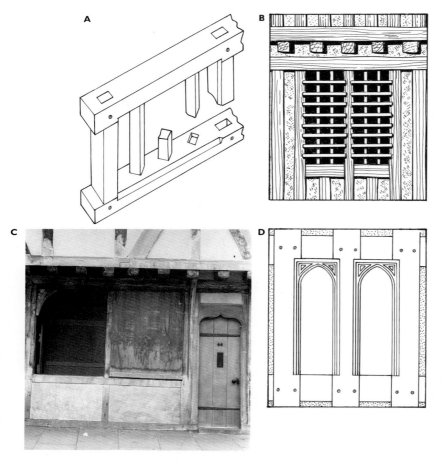

Windows

Surviving medieval windows are much rarer than entrances since they lacked glazing, and later generations found even more need to modernize them.

In timber and stone houses alike, windows were no more than openings, which, if they were of any size, were filled with square bars, or mullions, set edge on (A), to keep out intruders and perhaps to support oiled linen which provided some translucency. When these windows ventilated a service room which had to be kept cool, louvers might be set in front of the mullions (B).

Alternatively, the window might be designed for a shop where goods were displayed. In this case, it would have to be clear of bars, as in this restored window in a house in Church Street, Tewkesbury, now open as a museum (c). When the shop was closed, the window needed to be secured with strong shutters to make up for the lack of bars.

Decoration

The more important windows of even modest medieval houses might have moulded surrounds and mullions which continued into decorated heads in emulation of the grander windows of manor houses and churches. Rows of windows set between studs could have simple, pointed heads (D), but various forms of tracery made a more splendid show, as these windows from Salisbury (E), Oakham, Rutland (F), Bocking, Essex (G), and Royston, Hertfordshire (H), show.

Three very different windows in very different situations show the variety in even fairly plain openings: a large hall window with two tiers of openings with pointed heads at Langley, Kent (I); a small timber window with edge-on mullions set in the cob walls of a hall-house at Christow, Devon (J); and an internal window filled with lattice set in a house of mud and stud, which came from near Louth and has now been reconstructed at Church Farm Museum, Skegness (K).

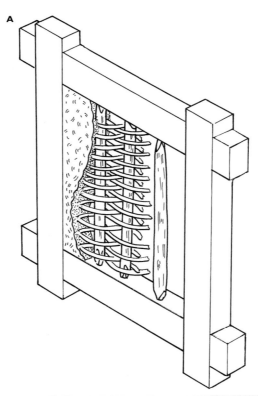

Walls

The panels of a timber-framed
building were usually filled with
wattle and daub. The wattles were
saplings or withies of hazel sprung
into grooves or small drill-holes in
the main timbers and then
interwoven with twigs or tendrils
(A). Sometimes a wooden lattice of
interwoven laths was used
instead. On top of this was worked
the daub, a mixture of earth, clay,
lime and animal dung, or
whatever was available, bound
with animal hair or strands of
vegetable matter such as straw.
Then came a layer of plaster for
protection which was limewashed
to make it waterproof (B).

In many ways this made a
very efficient wall: it was cheap
and had good insulation
properties, but it needed
maintenance, especially if the
frame moved slightly and caused
gaps to appear in the infilling.
Most movement in timber-framed
buildings was caused by the oak
drying out in the first few years

after construction, and later
movement is often the result of
unwise alteration to the frame.
Surprisingly, considering its
fragility, original wattle and daub
often survives.

Decoration

Both the plaster and the face of
the timber frame might be given
a coat of limewash for
waterproofing. This left the
surface a dead white, but various
natural colours might be washed
in, perhaps with a contrast
between the timbers and the
plaster.

North of London, around the
borders of Essex, Hertfordshire,
Cambridgeshire and Suffolk, it was
the practice to cover frame and
infilling alike with a thick coat of
plaster or pargetting, which might
then be patterned in various
ways. Panels of chequerwork (c)
and of intersecting arcs (D) were
commonly used, and braided and
herring-bone patterns can
sometimes be found both inside
and outside (E) and (F).

Inside the hall

The hall was the principal room of a medieval house, and this was true right through society from the king down to comparatively humble peasants. The smallest houses of the poorest peasants do not survive, but hall-houses belonging to the richer peasants of the last two centuries of the Middle Ages can be found around Britain to the tune of several thousand, albeit in an altered state. This selection shows the appearance of four halls as they might have been when new in the fifteenth century.

The grandest, though not the largest (A), was built in Worcestershire at Grafton Flyford, possibly by a clergyman, who had an important position in medieval society. This may explain its lavish use of heavy timbers to span the roof of the hall. They consist of a pair of short crucks, known as base-crucks, and carry a pair of massive tie-beams clamping the longitudinal roof timbers into position. The ties are supported by curved braces which form a graceful pointed arch, so giving the hall much of its status. At the far end there is a screen shielding the entrances on each side, and, beyond that, two doorways with ogee arches give access to a pair of service rooms.

Probably marginally larger, though notable for the use of comparatively slender timbers, is the box-framed hall of a Wealden house near Maidstone (B) which would have belonged to one of Kent's proverbially affluent yeomen. This view shows the typical roof of the south-east in which a single post, known as a crown-post, supports a lengthwise plate on which the roof collars rest, bracing the rafters pair by pair. A single doorway leads into the chamber at the high end. To the right of it the high table would have been placed, with a chair or two for the master and his wife in places of honour at the centre of the far side. Benches or stools for the rest of the household would have been set beside and opposite them.

Narrower and lower is the box-framed hall (C) at Coleshill, Warwickshire, which belonged to a more modest peasant, craftsman or trader. Nevertheless, the hall is framed in the Midlands way with heavier timbers, notably the collar halfway up the roof, and the longitudinal timbers, or purlins, it supports beneath the rafters.

A

Finally, comes a hall with a cruck-frame which once belonged to a relatively poor Worcestershire peasant who lived at Defford (D). The crucks provide an impressive interior to the hall. They were probably not just the most substantial timbers in the house, but the only substantial ones. It is more than likely that they were provided by the peasant's manorial landlord who was anxious to see his tenants well housed, if only to be sure of his rent. The free provision of the crucks gave the tenant an incentive to build well, and if his house did not outlast his tenancy, the crucks could be reclaimed by the landlord for re-use in another house.

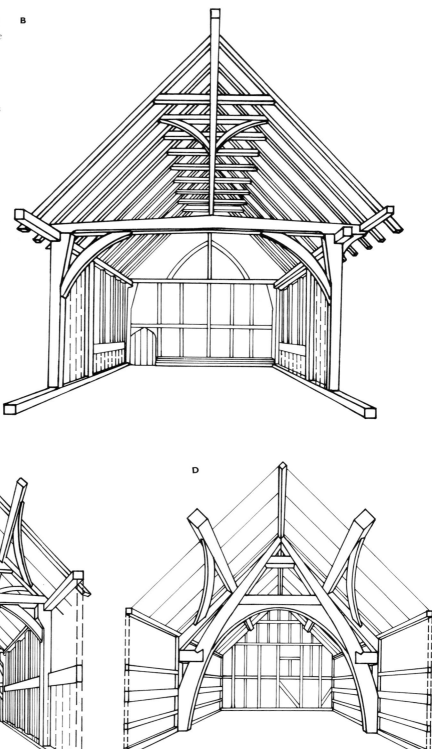

B

C

D

A

B

C

The hall and its details

Outside museum examples, few halls still remain open as they originally were, and those that do have been greatly altered. When the hall became obsolete in the sixteenth and seventeenth centuries, there was little incentive to preserve it as an entity in its own right, and in most cases a floor was inserted into it to divide it into an upper and a lower room. The upper room of a once open hall at Great Baddow, Essex (A), still has the ornate roof framing in its midst, now rather an impediment to movement, but impressive nonetheless. It plays an essential part in supporting the roof rafters.

The upper part of the cruck-frame of a hall at Condover, Shropshire (B), is equally impressive, and equally necessary for the support of the roof, but, being part of a dividing wall, it is less of an impediment. Unfortunately, doorways have been cut through the timbers and the full effect of the graceful arch formed by the crucks is lost.

The full appearance of these great spaces can only be seen in museum examples, like those at the Weald and Downland Open Air Museum at Singleton, near Chichester in West Sussex. One house there, Bayleaf, is a restored Wealden house originally built at Boughbeech in Kent. It is now complete with the high end of the hall (C) furnished with a table and benches, and the low end (D) opening into a cross-passage that runs between the front and back entrances, with the pair of arched doorways for the two service rooms beyond that.

The far smaller hall brought from Boarhunt in Hampshire has little more than bare essentials. The high end is marked by a single large window and a doorway into the chamber beyond it (E), while the low end (F) has no cross-passage and only a single entrance from outside, and a door into a single service room. Spanning the centre of the hall is a base-cruck truss, the one object of status, and unusual in a house as small as this. It also serves a more mundane function since an ordinary tie-beam linking the low walls would be a hazard to tall people.

Restoration

The main features of hall-houses which are still in use are never as clearly visible as they are in Bayleaf or the house from Boarhunt. Nevertheless, whatever remains is always worth conserving and can be restored when the opportunity presents itself. The windows, for instance, can sometimes be restored up to a point, although it is necessary to fit glass into whatever form of mullions are suggested by empty mortises in the timber above and beneath them. They may be fitted out with shutters, either suggested by surviving iron pivots which once carried hinged shutters, or by grooves which carried sliding shutters.

Sometimes it is possible to restore the shape of the doorways into the service rooms and the chamber. Oak doors constructed and hung in the medieval way can be fitted into them. Similarly, moulded timbers can be restored where they have been cut away, provided that enough of the original remains to copy.

To restore the hall is another matter. Apart from any other consideration, it usually involves structural changes, and nothing is more conducive to disaster in an old house than that.

D

E

F

Shutters, doors and doorways

Because medieval windows had no glass in them, most of the major ones had some means of securing them to keep out the weather and unwanted visitors. Hinged shutters were the commonest means of doing this, and hardly differed from doors. They were battened planks with iron strap hinges terminating in rings which dropped on to heavy vertical pivots spiked into the timbers on each side of the window. These pivots are often the only surviving evidence of shutters, which were usually removed when the windows were glazed. Smaller windows had shutters which slid in grooves cut into the timbers forming the base and the head of the window (A).

Vertical shutters

Occasionally vertically sliding shutters were used (B); these were similar in design and slid in grooves in the timbers on each side of the window, but had to be fastened shut with a strap or a peg, and simply dropped down to the bottom of the grooves when open. Because replacement windows often required new frames, these grooves are often obscured, if they have not been removed together with the timbers into which they were cut. The one timber that has a good chance of surviving is the plate

continued on p. 71

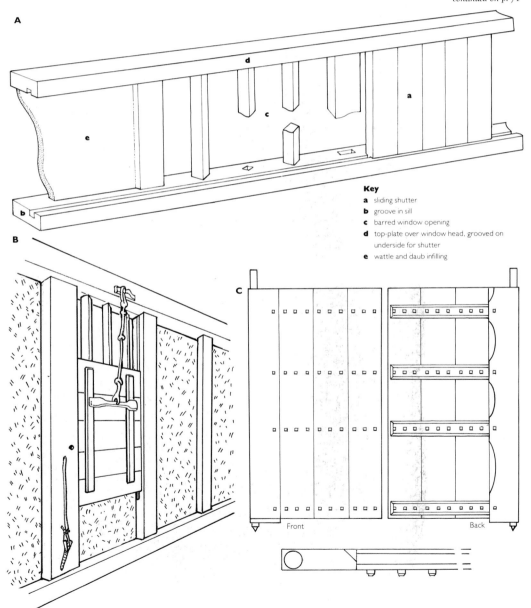

Key

a sliding shutter
b groove in sill
c barred window opening
d top-plate over window head, grooved on underside for shutter
e wattle and daub infilling

Front

Back

The Old Shop at Bignor in West Sussex is a much smaller version of Old Bell Farm. It is also less ornate, a reflection of the lesser affluence of West Sussex yeomen. The house is, nevertheless, of the Wealden type, with a central hall recessed between the jettied upper storeys over the chamber (to the left) and over the entrance passage and service rooms (to the right). The brick nogging in the central section probably replaces part of a large window that once provided light for the high table in the hall. There is a chimney-stack serving an enclosed fireplace instead of a formerly open hearth.

In much of the Middle Ages to have a house with upper storeys was a sign of wealth. Although jetties probably originated because this was the easiest way of fitting joists into a timber frame, they were an overt sign of an upper floor and consequently at the same time gave a house a modicum of status. The recessed hall and the way the eaves of the roof are carried in front of it by gracefully curved braces is a typical feature of Wealden halls such as this. There is some mystery surrounding the origin of their design. The first Wealden halls were probably built in the middle of the fourteenth century, but whether they were first built by ecclesiastical landlords or by the yeomen is not yet known.

continued from p. 68

which runs along the top of the wall and into which the window and its shutter fitted, so here is a good place to look for evidence when a later, decayed window is removed.

Doors and doorways

The doors of medieval peasant houses were usually formed out of three planks, nailed to battens top and bottom, although occasionally they might be more elaborate.

They were usually hung on iron ring and pivot hinges. Sometimes they were harr-hung (c, page 68), that is the inner vertical plank was made to extend upwards and downwards to form projecting circular pivots; the bottom pivot was engaged in a corresponding hole set in the timber threshold, while the top pivot was clasped inside the door lintel.

The internal doorways were often as decorated as the main entrance doorway. This was particularly true of the doorways in the hall which led into the chamber and the two service rooms. They might be simply chamfered and have pointed arches (D), or have an ogee arch (E). More elaborate doorways were on occasion splendidly carved, like the twin doorways into the service rooms at a late thirteenth-century farmhouse at Black Notley, Essex (F), which have deeply carved cusped foils set into the spandrels of their arched heads.

D

E

F

Coves and dais-beams

To mark the high table there was often an especially ornate beam set into the wall behind it. This originated in the lavish canopies which were important features of royal and aristocratic halls. Some farmhouses went as far as having a curved canopy or cove extending outwards from the wall. Just occasionally they were elaborately painted, some of which survive.

The Nine Worthies depicted on the panels of a cove at Great Binnal in Shropshire (A and B) are unique, but any surviving cove, such as the one at Edge in Gloucestershire (C), is a rarity. Floors have been inserted into both these halls, falsely suggesting that the coves were designed to support them, but the real function of coves was to provide notional protection for the high table and to draw attention to it and its occupants.

In Devon and other parts of the West Country it was common practice to allow the joists of the room over the chamber to project into the hall as an internal jetty (D), taking the place of a cove.

The most usual way of marking the high end of the hall was simply by an ornate dais-beam. In Bayleaf at the Weald

and Downland Open Air Museum, this beam simply has a hollow moulding carved into its lower edge, as though it were a cove in miniature (E). At a farm at Brook in Kent, the beam is more ornately moulded (F): the upper side is embattled as though it were a reminder of the military origins of the class of yeoman from which its owner perhaps believed he had sprung.

Sometimes the partition between the hall and the chamber beyond it was ornately panelled beneath the dais-beam. The panelling was often made up of planks set into grooved studs or muntins; sometimes the planks were carved with a central rib (G), rather like the linenfold motif used in the panels of grand houses at the end of the Middle Ages.

D

E

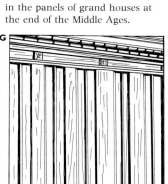

G

F

Carved decoration

Apart from coves and dais-beams, different parts of the hall might be decorated with carving, mostly in the form of the flattening or chamfering of the edges of the main timbers. Other carving was mostly confined to the principal roof timbers, but sometimes the posts forming the vertical sections of the main trusses were carved.

The early fourteenth-century hall of Edgar's Farm, re-erected at the Museum of East Anglian Life at Stowmarket, Suffolk, has fine capitals on octagonal posts, carved very much as they would have been in a stone church (A). A rather later farmhouse at Shillington in Bedfordshire has more elaborately carved capitals on the posts forming the central truss in the hall (B). The lower part of the cruck-truss in a farm at Barton-under-Needwood in Staffordshire has carved shafts and capitals just below where the crucks bow inwards to support the roof timbers (C).

Crown-posts

In East Anglia, Essex, and the south-east generally, the commonest place to find elaborate carving is on the so-called crown-post which rises from the centre of the tie-beam to support a longitudinal plate beneath the roof collars. The crown-post was carved in a number of ways with a base and capital in emulation of

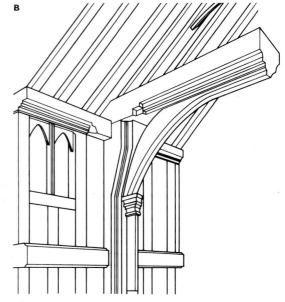

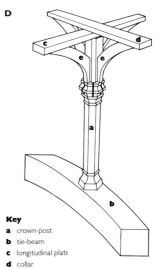

Key
a crown-post
b tie-beam
c longitudinal plate
d collar
e carved braces

the latest taste to be found in church architecture. Above the capital, curved braces radiated out to support the longitudinal plate and the collars it carried (D and E); sometimes it was carved with four projecting ribs which continued the flowing lines of the braces up and down (F).

Wind-braces
In the rest of the country, particularly the west, the Midlands and adjacent parts of

Wales, it was customary to carve the curved wind-braces which supported the longitudinal roof purlins of the more lavish halls and triangulated the principal rafters to stop them from leaning out of true. Their purpose was largely decorative. When the braces were carved with cusps, they produced patterns which rivalled the tracery in church windows (G), and made the grandest roofs of all.

The difficulty with all this roof

carving is that for the most part it is now invisible above the inserted floors and ceiling of later rooms. There are many practical reasons why the roofs cannot be opened up: they serve as dumps for forgotten household goods, as a place for water pipes and tanks, television aerials and electric cables, and as insulation for the rooms below. With all these cleared away, it is still difficult to open up a ceiling to make a once splendid roof visible.

G Roofs of Fiddleford Mill, Dorset

E

F

A

B

Cross-passages, stairs and privies

While the open hall of medieval houses can often be recognized only by the soot from the open fire which collected on the roof before a chimney-stack was built to enclose the hearth, the cross-passage, which led between the front and back doors and opened into the hall on one side, and into the service rooms by way of two doors on the other, often remains more or less intact. In this farmhouse built of cob at Norton Fitzwarren, Somerset (A), the possibility that it contains a hall is entirely unexpected from its outside appearance, but the front entrance opens into a cross-passage (B), so making the existence of the remains of its hall seem far more likely.

The upper rooms of hall-houses were subsidiary and mainly used as stores. There was consequently little point in having ornate staircases to reach them. Most hall-houses were therefore provided with hardly more than ladders, and various primitive types of stair sufficed (c). Blocks of wood supported by stout lengths of timber provided a strong stair which could carry the greatest weight of agricultural goods, such as the sacks of grain carried up to an upper room for storage.

Archaeological research shows that many medieval houses had outside privies nearby, just as they continued to do until this century. While people remained hardy and their numbers did not overburden what the soil and country streams could purify, there was little harm in this. The hypothetical privy (D) built out from an upper chamber of Bayleaf, the hall-house rebuilt at the Weald and Downland Open Air Museum, may show what was an unusual luxury for fastidious households.

C

D

Tudor and Jacobean houses

'I like well the old English . . . buyldinge where the roome is large and the chimney or herth, in the middest. Certainely thereby ill vapour and gnatts are kept out, lesse firinge [fuel] will serve the turne, and men had then more lusty and able bodies then they have now.' This was how the lawyer and mathematician Edward Howes nostalgically remembered the open hall-house of the Middle Ages when he wrote to his friend John Winthrop, the Governor of Massachusetts, in 1632 about the new houses of their times.

Perhaps there is some comfort in knowing that the imagined values of the good old days have attracted people throughout history. Yet it is strange that Howe so readily criticized the innovations of the sixteenth and seventeenth centuries. While he was certainly right in saying that the new enclosed chimney-stacks caused fires to burn more quickly, and there is no doubt that they brought draughts and concentrated the heat so that one's face could burn and one's back freeze, the convenience of an enclosed hearth was overwhelming, gnats or no gnats. Enclosed hearths were cleaner and facilitated cooking, and they were there to stay. Add to them newly glazed windows, and houses could be made warmer and more comfortable. Draughts might be concentrated, but draughts were not everywhere in the room.

With the continuous upper floor from end to end that the chimney-stack made possible, a house could be planned with a single staircase so that its space was better utilized than before. This was as well because these innovations coincided with a period of great affluence among yeomen and merchants which allowed them to fill their houses with valuable fixtures and fittings.

While these developments affected the inside of the house most, the outside did not remain unchanged by them. Old forms were carried to new peaks of achievement, and new forms were added to them. Timber-framing enjoyed a last fling, made all the more exciting by its exuberant decoration. Brick and masonry added a new sense of quality and status to the appearance of houses.

To have a chimney-stack and the continuous upper storey it made possible were novelties that should be advertised. In some parts of the country, especially in the south-east and East Anglia where the brick-making industry was advancing rapidly, the brick stack gave builders a new opportunity for a show of decoration. Decorated shafts of many ingenious kinds with oversailing courses of bricks capping the top made a splendid show, all to impress the onlooker that here was a house which was thoroughly up to date.

The base of the stack might have an inset panel with the owner's initials inscribed on it together with those of his wife and the date, so that no one need be ignorant of who was responsible for introducing the new features. In the later years of Queen Elizabeth it rapidly became the height of fashion to inscribe dates of new houses, either here on the chimney, on a panel over the front door or in some other prominent position. This incidentally was not just an English fashion, but one that swept all Europe at the end of the sixteenth century and has continued ever since.

The construction of the house changed a little too, as new decorative forms of timber-framing made their appearance. A continuous upper floor was often advertised by allowing it to oversail the ground floor so that everyone could see it. At the same time the projecting or jettied ends of the floor joists might have a fashionably carved fascia beam attached to them as an extra mark of status.

Slowly the classical forms revived by the Italian Renaissance reached England, mostly through illustrations in architectural books such as the ones published by the Italian architect Sebastiano Serlio and the Lowlanders Wendel Ditterlin and Vredeman de Vries. Nevertheless, Tudor and Jacobean taste did not immediately reflect the formal rules of classicism. Instead, it was particularly fanciful, and showed overtones of the more chivalrous aspects of the past; much of this classical decoration was capriciously applied and notably imaginative, the purity of classical form invariably bowing to the fantastic.

The result was that the front of a particularly wealthy yeoman's or merchant's house might have a door surround decorated with classical columns, but, for the rest, it could be built up with jettied floors piled one on another to carry jettied gables over them. The jetties could be given fantastically carved brackets, not so much for support as for additional emphasis. Similarly, projecting oriel windows again satisfied the desire for a lively front and added yet more carved decoration and, with it, more status to a house. Meanwhile the rules of order and proportion implied by the classical columns were forgotten in the exuberance of the rest.

Windows rapidly became objects of status in their own right. As glass became cheap enough towards the end of the sixteenth century to enable yeomen and merchants to buy it for their houses, it became a sign of wealth to increase the number of windows far beyond what the needs of practicality required. Many timber houses were consequently given long bands of what were called clerestory windows, which might even stretch right across the front of a house, the only breaks being where the timber posts of the frame passed through them. The main rooms would be marked by large deep windows, stretching down to a lower level or projecting outwards as oriels. Indeed some houses had so much glass that even the 'sun-trap' houses of the Modern Movement in the 1930s had little more. There was a difference. In the 1930s plenty of sunlight inside a house was believed to bring health, and white and light colours prevailed: they were cleaner. In the sixteenth and seventeenth centuries sunlight brought a warm glow to the opulent colourful decorations and furnishings that were all the rage. Wealth, not health, was the keynote.

The 1930s houses of course had large panes of glass as well as large windows, though unwisely they were set in steel frames which quickly rusted, whereas the old timber houses had very small panes of glass, seldom more than 6 inches overall. They were set either square or diamond-wise in lead frames or cames that did not rust and readily allowed a pane of glass to be replaced if it was broken, but this does not mean that Tudor and Jacobean windows survive in great numbers. By the eighteenth century large quantities of glass were no longer admired, and so the long bands of glass were blocked, the oriels removed and replaced by smaller sash windows of a different, more fashionable shape. The lead cames were melted down for gutters, and wooden frames with classical proportions replaced them.

During the seventeenth century, timber dropped slowly out of favour as a building material for the frame of a house. Brick or stone, depending on local supplies, was more estimable, and by 1700 was cheaper too for the entire carcase, so far had the cultivation of building timber declined and the production of brick kilns and stone quarries grown.

One consequence was that it was hard to fit large areas of glass into what was now a structural wall, and windows, both individually and in groups, became smaller and increasingly took on classical proportions. Where brick was the dominant building material, window frames were, nevertheless, usually made of timber, and had vertical and horizontal bars, mullions and transoms, dividing them up and supporting the lead cames, and also the brickwork above them. Where stone predominated, the mullions and transoms were often also of stone, and the windows were mostly arranged in horizontal bands, divided only by mullions that were moulded in the same way as the rest of the frame.

Some individual windows were set in wrought-iron frames and vertically hinged to open outwards as casements. The hinges and especially the catches provided the ironsmith with an opportunity for a decorative flourish or two, as did door hinges and catches. Again, these windows dropped out of fashion in the eighteenth century and could be replaced by newer, more fashionable ones even more easily.

Doors became more elaborate, but were still made in much the same way as before, even while their hinges, catches and locks took on the extravagant forms of the age. Once through the front door, however, the changes in the Tudor and Jacobean house became more apparent.

Interiors

No longer was the entry directly into the hall or into a screened passage that led directly into the hall. To be fair, in the north direct entry into the hall or firehouse did remain. Emily Brontë's Mr Lockwood, who was used to southern ways, found this very peculiar when he first visited Wuthering Heights on the Yorkshire Pennines; but in the rest of the country the entry was increasingly into a vestibule or lobby which gave the individual rooms a bit more privacy than in the past, and cut down draughts indoors.

Everywhere, except in the poorest houses, it was becoming more common to see the ground floors paved with brick, tile or stone flags which could more easily be kept clean. As the custom of digging out cellars beneath the house spread, floors were raised above the ground on joists and boarded, and this was done more often even if there were no cellars beneath. What had been common practice upstairs from the beginning slowly became universal. The edges of the beams and joists which supported the upper floors provided an opportunity for chamfers or elaborate carved mouldings, and, where these timbers came to an end, the chamfers or mouldings could stop with a decorative carved scroll. Even in modest houses the undersides of the joists supporting the floors over the chamber and service rooms are often chamfered and end in plain but pretty stops in the form of a single or double curve. The planked floors themselves not only had a flatter, permanent surface which could be easily cleaned, but they were warmer and drier into the bargain. As old trees which could provide very wide planks became harder to find, floor boards slowly decreased in width to 9 inches and less, so making them less prone to warping.

Another change was in the finish of walls. Increasingly, the frame and the plastered panels between its timbers were covered over. This might be with painted cloths, or the walls themselves might be plastered and painted as they had been in the past. Architectural patterns and rustic scenes took their place alongside the older abstract and naturalistic patterns of the Middle Ages. Panelling, or wainscotting as it was once called, also descended to the level of the smaller house.

Generally, panelling consisted of small, plain panels of thin wood, seldom more than about one foot square, set in a grooved frame with mouldings scratched or more carefully cut into its sides. The panels might be thicker away from where their edges fitted into the grooves of the frame, and then could be carved into patterns such as linenfold or, more classically, have their edges cut back with regular mouldings to produce a rectangular raised or fielded central area. At the top and bottom of the panels, more boldly carved planks formed a cornice beneath the ceiling, and skirting where the wall joined the floor. Further boldly carved timbers, sometimes with fanciful representations of the classical orders, divided the panelling into vertical sections. Like painted cloths and even the glazing of windows, panelling was considered to be a fitting, not a fixture, so, when a house changed hands, it would be removed. Much Elizabethan and Jacobean panelling looks as though it was not made for the house in which it is now found, and that is usually the case.

The ceilings remained much as before, although the open roof of the hall was increasingly despised, and only lofts remained for long without some form of ceiling. The undersides of ceiling beams and joists were now often carved with ornate mouldings, and sometimes they were painted and gilded. Nevertheless this opportunity to provide yet more decoration in a room slowly gave way to ceilings which were flat and plastered in the modern way. It was the plaster rather than the timber beams that received the decoration now, with various kinds of applied naturalistic patterns and abstract shapes rather like those used outside when a house was pargetted. This form of decoration was to come into its own later, when the dark wood and primary colours that the Elizabethans so liked had given way to lighter and less obtrusive tints.

The enclosed hearth

The newest feature of these houses was the enclosed hearth. The fireplace was therefore accentuated by various kinds of decoration, at least in the most important rooms. While the stack in a kitchen might be supported by a plain timber beam or bressummer over the hearth, in a parlour or when there was only one hearth in the house, this bressummer might be carved in the same way as a door lintel to suggest an arch. Some beams were carved with their owner's initials and a date. Grander houses had brick or stone arches over the hearth, and these could be moulded. The grandest houses had either columns or figures in the form of caryatids to support a form of classical entablature. Occasionally a naïve version of this idea came to be used for the fireplaces in a merchant's or yeoman's house.

The space between the arch and the ceiling, the overmantel, was often singled out for decoration, again just as it was in grand houses. Here there might be plaster figures, a rustic scene, heraldic or mythical animals, or a timber panel carved with grotesque arches of an exuberant but hardly correct classical type.

The hearth remained open and in some parts of the country was so large a space that people could sit in it. In the north the chimney was usually in the form of a timber-framed hood, plastered to make it fireproof. It covered a space called an ingle that might measure 6 by 10 feet or more. On one side it would be lit by a small window known as a fire-window; on the other it would be sheltered from the draughts of the front door or a passage leading to another room by a screen known as a heck. Often the ingle was large enough to contain built-in benches; here a family could draw up chairs as well. In Cumbria they customarily wore hats when sitting in the ingle because sooty rain came down the chimney.

Nearly all timber firehoods have now been replaced by brick or stone stacks, but the ovens and warm cupboards that were set into the backs of many chimney-stacks above the hearth do often survive and come to light when an old fireplace is opened up. Ovens were little more than large, round chambers up to 3 feet in diameter, and most of them were blocked up when they fell out of use. The warm cupboards were for storing salt, spices and dried fruit. They had doors which provided an opportunity for carving, with dates and initials taking their place beside intertwined braiding and naturalistic forms. In a few parts of the country, notably in the west, a larger chamber set beside the hearth shows where meat was hung to cure in smoke, either drawn off the main fire or produced by scorching wood shavings in a subsidiary fire. The purpose was to cure the meat but not to cook it, so the chamber could not be subject to the direct heat of the fire.

When coal became readily available for domestic fires in the eighteenth and nineteenth centuries, the wide, deep hearths of the past that were designed for large logs and heaps of glowing embers became redundant and so were blocked up. Small fireplaces designed to contain modest amounts of hot coals were put in their place. Sometimes these are so modern or have themselves been removed, for instance, with the advent of central heating, that it is worthwhile to open up the old hearth. There is always a risk: many open hearths were blocked up for the secondary reason that the wood fires had already so calcified the bricks around them that they had to be rebuilt anyway, and the restorer is left with a ruinous hole.

The hearth itself had irons to support logs and also cooking utensils. The number and type of irons multiplied, with some set in the base of the chimney to support hanging pots or spits that could be turned by little windmills caught by the uprush of hot air. Sometimes these irons had decorative flourishes wrought into their ends, like everything else the smith wrought.

The staircase, though not as new as an enclosed hearth, again received its share of decoration. In the Middle Ages a stair was little more than a ladder, and might be no more than solid, squared timbers supported on diagonal beams joining two floors. As soon as upper floors were important enough for the master and his visitors to use them, something more elaborate was needed. The stair itself was made from separate planks forming the treads and risers. These were fixed into planks called strings that rise diagonally between the floors with their faces set vertically. The underside edge of the string could be moulded, and the upper side, on the outer face of a stair, carried balusters and a rail. The balusters were often carved with grotesquely conceived classical forms, and might even be in the form of carved panels, but during the seventeenth century they increasingly took the form of turned pillars combining series of rings with convex and concave forms. Early rails were heavy and moulded along their sides, and, as the shape of the balusters was refined and lightened, they too were made slimmer.

The houses of the sixteenth and seventeenth centuries fill the countryside in a way that their medieval predecessors do not – at least outside Kent. Many of them are based on a medieval timber frame, even so, but all of them show how a prosperous yeomanry afforded the most modern amenities, thanks to the increasing affluence of their time. The main innovations – enclosed hearths, glazed windows and continuous upper floors – brought a series of house plans into existence that were never to be surpassed by later ones so far as the countryside was concerned. They suited all sizes of house, all classes of men and women. They could be used equally with or without a separate class of servants, and this has important implications for today. They embraced a number of good-sized rooms that were meant to be adaptable as well as comfortable, and these qualities remain. Never before had there been such variety in the houses of ordinary people, and this was not to be repeated until the Victorian age; but, by then, the population was ten times as great. There were to be no advances in planning in the eighteenth and nineteenth centuries, the same old plans being dressed in new styles until the irregularities of the Picturesque made their appearance, and these were of no particular benefit to easy living. Once brick and stone had made their appearance, there were to be no advances in constructional techniques either. In some ways houses were to be become less solidly built thereafter. All this applied to the countryside. In towns it was a different matter. Urban conditions required something else, but it was not until towns started to grow with a vengeance after the Great Fire of London in 1666 that significant advances in planning occurred there.

A

B

C

D

E

F

New plans

The sixteenth century and most of the seventeenth century brought great affluence to many English yeomen and enabled perhaps half the population to live far enough above subsistence level to devote time and money to their houses. What the yeomen of Kent had achieved in the last two centuries of the Middle Ages became widespread.

The triple innovations of enclosed hearths in chimney-stacks, continuous upper floors, and glazed windows made the open hall a thing of the past. More than that, the new wealth of countrymen liberated their powers of invention, which resulted in the greatest possible variation in the appearance of their houses. This affected the plans of their houses, the materials they used in building them, and the decoration they applied to them.

For a start, there were the new plans. These variously allowed for a hearth passage, a lobby entry, a heck entry, a central vestibule, or a double pile. Then there was an increasing range of materials. Timber-framing continued to flourish until the middle of the seventeenth century, but construction in brick or stone, depending on the resources of each locality, was quickly increasing.

The decorative qualities of timber-framing continued to be exploited, especially in the north and west, with ever more exuberant patterns. The arts of masonry and bricklaying also made a strong contribution of their own to decoration.

In the south-east close-studding remained the norm for timber-framed houses, but these could be distinguished from their forebears by the brick chimney-stacks that rose within them and the continuous upper floors that the enclosed hearths made possible. Upper floors were often emphasized by a jetty running along the entire front, as in this house at Westham, East Sussex (A). Where the money ran to it, a carved fascia added decoration to the status brought by a jetty.

TUDOR AND JACOBEAN HOUSES **85**

Lobby-entry plans

The house at Westham continued with plans that had evolved from the arrangements of the medieval hall-house, but the lobby-entry house with its aligned entrance and chimney-stack was significantly new. The oldest lobby-entry houses in the country were built in the first quarter of the sixteenth century, such as this one at Plaxtol, Kent (B), but this radical plan was slow to take root. Most lobby-entry houses were built well after Queen Elizabeth I came to the throne in 1558. They then became popular wherever timber-framing was still in use.

In the south-east, the plan was used for large houses as well, for instance in a grand house at Chiddingstone, Kent (C). Here, the house is framed with small panelling of close-studding, which by the end of the sixteenth century had at last gone out of fashion. It also has a fine range of glazed windows, designed to show the world that its builder was able to afford this innovation in full measure, as well as to let in plenty of light without the inconvenience of draughts.

By the seventeenth century, if not before, the lobby-entry plan had reached Yorkshire, as an early clothier's house at Worsbrough shows (D); here it is the characteristic northern love of diagonal studding to make up a herringbone pattern that gives the house its special character.

Building materials

The materials of the future, nevertheless, were brick and stone. The hearth-passage plan that directly descended from the old cross-passage plan of the medieval hall-house was adapted for stone houses right across the country from Dorset to Yorkshire, wherever there was good building stone.

Although the use of a central chimney-stack, detached from the exterior walls of the lobby-entry house, was not a sensible adaptation when it came to building houses in brick or stone, this did happen because the plan had become fashionable and the materials brought status. A

farmhouse built all of good local red brick at Greasby in Cheshire, in about 1680, shows this well (E).

A better way of planning a house of brick or stone was to build the stacks into the end walls, thus leaving the centre free for a vestibule running from the front door to a staircase and a back door or a rear service room. Houses with this pattern started to become popular in the seventeenth century, for example in a farmhouse at Bishopstone in Wiltshire (F), which appears quite different because of its prominent front gables, a local speciality.

Double-pile plans

Larger houses where four rooms were wanted on each floor often took the form of the double pile, with a room in each corner and usually with a central entrance vestibule and staircase. The earlier double piles were less regularly planned, but the rising classical

taste of the seventeenth century soon turned towards symmetry, as at a house at Wicken Bonhunt, Essex (G), which was extensively rebuilt to give it a double-pile plan.

Meanwhile in poor parts of the country, such as the marshland of Lancashire and the fenland and the Wolds of Lincolnshire, houses were still built of mud in various forms, using old-established plans with little more than lofts if they had an upper storey at all. There are one or two of these houses left in Formby in Lancashire as reminders of how the peasantry commonly lived on the marshy carrs below the Pennine foothills, and there are several more houses like this in Lincolnshire, notably at Mareham-le-Fen (H) and on the Wolds at Thimbleby. They are small and low—although not below today's standards for space—and their earthen walls are better insulation against the cold than many modern materials.

G

H

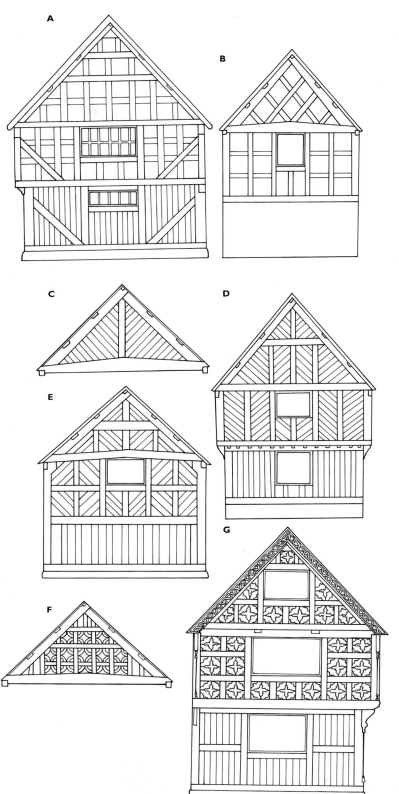

Decorative framing

The late sixteenth and early seventeenth centuries saw the most elaborate decoration of many features of the English house, a sure reflection of the widespread affluence of those days, and people's enjoyment of it.

This was the Indian summer of timber-framing, and timber houses were as elaborately finished as any other. Not only might each storey be jettied, but each might be treated with a different form of framing, for instance the close-studding of the late Middle Ages on one storey, and very small panels on the next (A); or small panels set horizontally below the gable and diagonally within it (B). The gable might be filled with a series of diagonal braces to form tiers of Vs, either upright (C), or upside down, and these could be elaborated all over the façade into a dazzling herringbone pattern (D), or a series of diamonds (E).

Finally, and the most ornamental of all, the façade could be filled with small panels, each of which was then given tiny curved braces (F), or cusped braces (G), making a series of roundels or stars. In the second of these two examples, the roof projects far enough beyond the gable to be finished by a pair of verge or bargeboards, another opportunity for rich carving. But these features rarely survive because it was their purpose to stop the rainwater running under the roof, and so they were prone to weather quickly and decay.

Pargetting

Pargetting remained popular north of London, and patterns in raised plaster as well as incised into it became more and more fanciful (H, page 89). Much of this carving and plastering has been destroyed. By its nature and position, it was at risk from the elements, and when timber-framed buildings finally fell out of fashion in the eighteenth century, they were sometimes tile-hung, which meant that battens had to be nailed to their frames, destroying much decoration in the process.

continued on page 89

A house at Betley, Staffordshire, which clearly shows its framed construction based on pairs of heavy, curved timbers known as crucks. The origin of this seemingly primitive form of construction is a matter of controversy, and it is not helped by the peculiar distribution of crucks, which are never found in the south-east and east of England. The further wing of the house is more normally framed with vertical posts and horizontal beams, but the way the frame is divided into a number of square panels is a typical sight in the West Midlands.

The enclosed hearth immediately became a new object of status and was therefore decorated to emphasize it. At Cobbe's Hall, Aldington, Kent (RIGHT), the timber bressummer is carved with a Tudor rose at one end and an Aragonese pomegranate at the other, as well as some fernleaf decoration suggesting a shallow arch; these probably refer to the period of Henry VIII's marriage to Catherine of Aragon and so help to date the building to the second or third decade of the sixteenth century. Above the beam, the plastered chimney-breast has some rare painted decoration in the form of intersecting arcs. The hearth itself has been modernized and given a stove, but during restoration a niche and the opening of an oven were discovered, suggesting that the hearth was originally used for cooking.

Even in a diminished form, the hall continued to dominate the planning of houses until the seventeenth century. When Doghurst Cottage was built at South Nutfield, Surrey (BELOW), in the sixteenth century it had a hall in the centre of the house, marked by the largest window. But instead of an open hearth, it was given an enclosed fireplace with a chimney-stack built against its rear wall. This just shows above the ridge of the roof, which is covered with local sandstone tiles of a type generically known as Horsham slates.

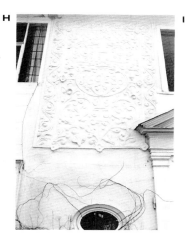

continued from page 86

Further ruination came when plastered buildings were given heavy coats of hard stucco to bring them into line with the taste of the late eighteenth and early nineteenth centuries. Even when patterned pargetting survives, generations of repainting have usually left it obscured beneath successive coats of limewash; but at least that is better than when it has been left exposed so the patterns are almost worn away.

Timber carving

Sometimes principal timbers could be carved, such as dragon posts (I), and posts at corners or framing windows (J). Carved timberwork reached its height in the West Midlands, for instance in the prominent gable of a farm at Knockin in Shropshire (K), or at the command of prosperous merchants and court officials, such as the one who was probably responsible for rebuilding this former house at Ludlow in Shropshire (L), now The Feathers.

Brickwork

Bricks became progressively cheaper in the sixteenth and seventeenth centuries. The art of brickmaking was probably lost in Britain after the collapse of the Roman Empire in the fifth century, and only in the later Middle Ages was it revived to compete with imported bricks from the Low Countries. Where there were good deposits of clay or brick-earth, notably in the south-east, Essex and East Anglia, and parts of the Midlands and north, home-made bricks were already as cheap as timber for house building by the middle of the seventeenth century, and they became even cheaper.

At first, bricks were generally longer and wider than modern ones, and shallower too. They lacked the indented top or frog that in later bricks held the mortar. The bricks were laid randomly, some stretching along the wall, others across it showing their heads on the outside face (A). When bricklayers imposed some order on the coursing of bricks, they adopted the ancient practice of laying courses of lengthwise bricks or stretchers, and courses of crosswise bricks or headers (B), eventually in alternate courses. This came to be known as English bond (C).

Mortar

Bricks were joined with mortar, a mixture of sand and lime that varied, depending on local supplies. When dry, it remained softer than the bricks or, for that matter, the stone it held in place. It had to be pointed to bring it close to the edge of the bricks or stones so that it would keep water penetration to a minimum, but it had to be left slightly recessed so that it did not allow water to build up in the brick or stone. If that were to happen, there would be excessive decay, and, with frost, there would be cracking as well.

Soft mortars have the advantage of allowing the brick or stone to move slightly, while hard, modern cement mortars put excessive pressure on various points of the brickwork or masonry and cause all kinds of trouble. Worst of all is the pointing of inexperienced builders who use cement and allow the mortar either to project in a web of hard lines or to slop over the bricks or masonry in an unsightly mess. In both cases, this puts the

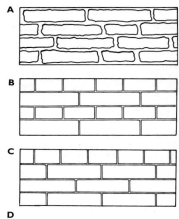

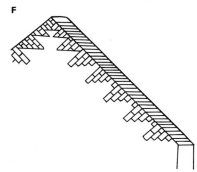

bricks or stones at risk by letting rainwater penetrate them.

Moulding and firing

The firing process left bricks a rosy pink, but colours varied and some bricks were allowed to become vitrified, giving them a shiny bluish appearance. This gave bricklayers the opportunity of making patterns in their brickwork, notably a chequerwork of dark bricks on light ones, or a diaper of intersecting diagonal lines, such as can be seen on several houses in the Leicestershire village of Barsby (D).

Fine bricks could be moulded into various shapes before firing, or carved or rubbed into shape afterwards. They might then be used for door surrounds, window frames, eaves, decorative chimney-stacks and many other features.

With the introduction of architectural books from France and the Low Countries in the later sixteenth century, illustrating the forms inspired by Renaissance Italy, builders slowly built up a corpus of classical decoration which they could apply to their own houses.

This form of decoration was given great impetus by Inigo Jones, the first architect in England who thoroughly understood classical architecture. By the 1630s, bricklayers were copying these forms in a haphazard way, for instance in south London at Croom's Hill, Greenwich (E).

The pilasters and pedimented gables of this house had only a little to do with classical architecture, but gables of all kinds were widespread in the

brick houses of Lowland and Baltic towns, and they soon became fashionable in the eastern counties of England. One way of completing the brickwork of a plain gable was to 'tumble' the bricks immediately beneath the gable (F) to make the necessary angle. Another way, common in the Baltic, was to let each course of bricks project, so forming a crow-step gable, like one on a house built in about 1613 at Freiston in Lincolnshire (G). The more shapely double curves of a farmhouse at Huntingfield in Suffolk (H) were only rivalled by the combination of curves and pediment, seen here at Caythorpe in Lincolnshire (I) and Guilton in Kent (J). These forms remained fashionable right to the end of the seventeenth century, as these houses show.

G

H

I

J

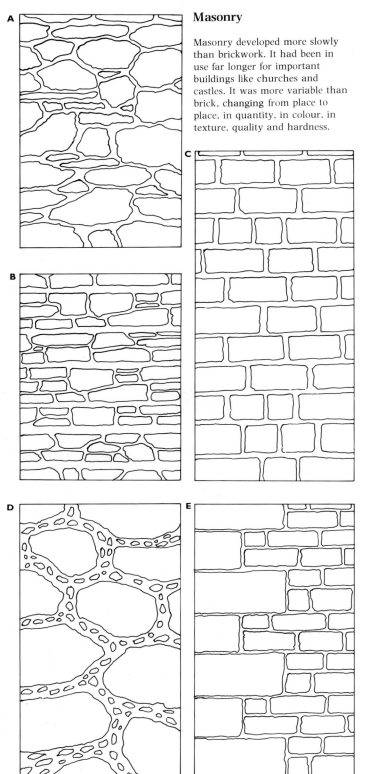

Masonry

Masonry developed more slowly than brickwork. It had been in use far longer for important buildings like churches and castles. It was more variable than brick, changing from place to place, in quantity, in colour, in texture, quality and hardness.

Except where it was freely available, it was always held in higher esteem than brick.

Yeomen and lesser men could not always afford more than rough blocks of stone or rubble, laid quite irregularly (A), or brought only into rough courses (B), and only the best stone, such as the fine Jurassic limestone of the Cotswolds, could be cheaply cut into rectangular blocks and laid in regular courses (C). All rough blocks of stone needed large quantities of mortar to fill the gaps between them, and so, in some places, to reduce the amount of mortar and to produce a decorative effect small chips of stone were inserted, a practice known as galletting (D).

At its corners, a building needed regularly cut, good-quality stone or, failing that, bricks to provide a strong finish, a method known as quoining (E). Poor stone could be rendered over with mortar to protect it and to hide its rough appearance. In a later age this would be lined to suggest superior masonry.

Watershot masonry is a speciality of the Pennines and the north (F). The courses of stones are set at a slightly downward angle to reduce water penetration into the masonry, giving the wall an odd, stepped apperance.

Gables

The ornate gables and the Dutch gables of the eastern counties were seldom built in stone, if only because there was no stone in those counties. This type of gable did not become fashionable in the west or north where good stone abounded. Traditional gables remained popular here until well into the eighteenth century, not just to finish roofs at each end, but as features in their own right. They gave a house the varied outline that became increasingly fashionable in the sixteenth and seventeenth centuries. House builders, in Gloucestershire particularly, favoured gables, which are inseparable from the traditions of the Cotswolds. Here there was plenty of good stone to use, as a fine farmhouse at Kings Stanley shows (G).

F

G

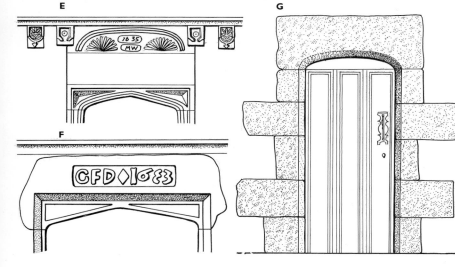

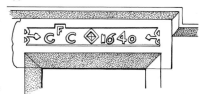

Entrance doors

The forms of arched entrance adapted for the timber houses of yeomen at the end of the Middle Ages continued into the sixteenth and seventeenth centuries, changing only imperceptibly under the influence of Renaissance classicism or as they came to be built in stone.

Porches

One of the most sensible innovations, considering the English climate, was the use of porches. They had already had a long history among grander houses, but now they became commoner among lesser ones. Even in a comparatively modest house, a porch might take the form of an open timber-framed structure with a small room over it. A particularly grand porch of this type (A) belongs to a fairly modest house of 1599 in Bromley, south London, and its upper storey accommodates a small room that may once have been an office. The upper part of the porch had its timbers turned in the form of the fashionable balusters of the period. Over half a century later, stone porches were still being built in the north in medieval forms, so far were they behind the south in matters of fashion.

Seventeenth-century brick porches in the south often mixed medieval and classical motifs in the way shown by one at Abinger in Surrey (B), and a stone porch at Sulgrave in Northamptonshire, which is dated 1636, is still innocent of classical influence (c).

Door frames

Many fantastically decorated doorheads appeared at this time, especially in the north. One at Humby in Lincolnshire of 1631 (D) is unusual for both the county where it is found and its

peculiarly stylized forms; the
upper part of one at Dacre in the
Yorkshire Dales (E), dated only
four years later, shows the way
that the decoration of doorheads
in the Dales was going to take
later in the century. Generally
they kept to medieval forms (F), or
ventured only as far as an oval
'basket' arch (G), or some minimal
Jacobean carving in the hard
stone of the area (H). Doorheads
were just as old-fashioned, if not
more so, in Wales, in both stone
doorways (I) and timber ones (J).

The door frames, whether of
stone or timber, had their edges
moulded or at least chamfered to
reduce the sharp edge and provide
more decoration; near the ground,
these mouldings or chamfers
stopped in a carved flourish, again
reminiscent of the decoration
found in late Gothic churches (K).

The doors themselves were still
made of vertical planks of wood,
and advanced little beyond their
medieval predecessors. Stronger
doors were battened both
crossways and up and down, and
held with heavy iron studs rather
than nails (L); interior doors were
generally lighter.

Hinges

The large iron hinges used on
doors, both inside and out, gave
the ironsmith an opportunity for
practising his skill in decoration.
He could work their ends into all
kinds of fanciful patterns, such as
hearts, fleurs-de-lis (M) or
cocksheads. Similarly, bolts and
catches were wrought and
hammered into decorative
patterns, but being constantly
handled, these had to be more
practical (N).

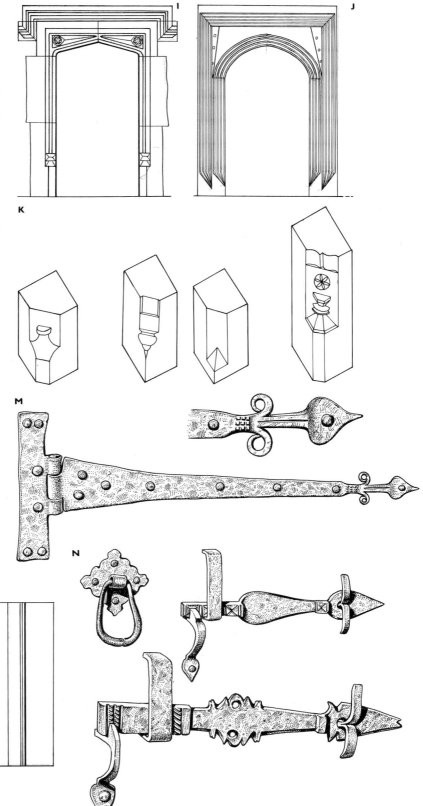

Windows

Although the glazing of windows with panes of glass made a radical difference to the comfort of a room, the first window frames were little different from their unglazed medieval predecessors. The grooved lead bars or cames which held the panes of glass were set in a wooden frame still divided vertically by plain mullions. These were now grooved to take the cames, and the narrower, edge-on bars were used to support the cames, which were tied to them with lead wire. Soon, however, the mullions were decorated with inset chamfers or rounded mouldings (A), and these became popular in various forms all round the country, in frames of both timber and stone. The various mouldings used for mullions differed from place to place, depending on local traditions and taste.

Because the walls of timber-framed houses were not structural, windows could stretch along them from end to end, and, for reasons of status more than the needs of illumination, they often did so. Similarly, it was comparatively easy to make windows project in the form of oriels, especially when they were set beneath the eaves or a jetty. Oriel windows could be supported either by carved brackets (B), or moulded beams (C). This was another way of making windows more prominent and drawing attention to them.

Where stone became the main building material, there was less scope for either long bands of windows or highly carved frames. The windows weakened the structural wall into which they were set, and the frames therefore needed the support of strong mullions to make up for this. Stone carving was itself expensive since it needed good-quality stone, even in places like north-west Dorset (D) where it could be easily cut, and it needed skilled craftsmanship as well. In the Pennines, where the hard stone resisted equally the rough weather and the mason's chisel, the plain bands of mullions were nearly all the decoration a window received.

They were not quite all, though. Most windows in stone houses were given a projecting carved moulding above them to throw off the rainwater and stop it from dripping on to the window itself. The ends of these drip-moulds were again often decorated, and in the Pennines this carving competed with the carved doorheads in its elaboration (E).

Only the occasional window frame was made to open, and these were almost invariably made of wrought iron. They were hinged at one side and fastened at the other. The catches that fastened them shut and, to a lesser extent, the casement pulls and stays that used to keep them

open gave the smith a good opportunity to express his considerable skills (F).

Glass
The vulnerability of glass and the lead cames that carried it means that even fragments of original windows of this period are rare. Sometimes enough fragments may remain to indicate how a restoration could be made. Apart from the possible destruction of later but rather more useful types of window, such as Georgian sashes, there is one major difficulty in this restoration: the glass itself. Early glass was either blown into a cylinder which was then cut lengthwise and flattened before being cut into panes, or it was spun into a disc before being

cut. In either case, the glass itself was seldom very clear, and suffered from discolouration and internal bubbling and striation. The boss at the centre of a piece of spun glass was seldom used unless translucency rather than transparency was the only object.

Old glass cannot be found in useful quantities, and so any reproduction must find a compromise, as it must in all restorations. The advantages of modern clear glass need to be weighed against the failings of old glass even though these gave it character. What is certain is that the lumpiness and colouration of so-called bottle glass do not look as ancient as its admirers hope, and only reproduce the character of the tea shoppe.

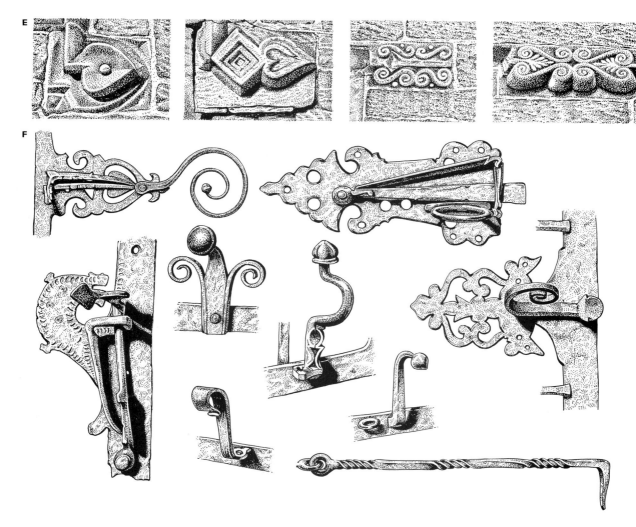

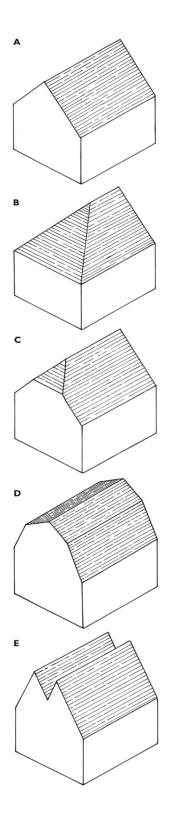

Roofs

In the Middle Ages roofs followed two basic forms. More commonly they were pitched with a ridge running from end to end to terminate in a gable (A); alternatively the ends might be pitched as well to join the main slopes at an angle known as a hip (B), a form that was particularly favoured in Kent. The gabled roof had the advantage of simpler carpentry; the hipped roof had the advantage of the stability given to it by the buttressing effect of the end slopes.

With the arrival of upper storeys and garrets, the roof space came to be used for storage, but, since windows could not easily be fitted into a hipped roof, the half-hipped form was used, particularly in the south-east, to get the best of both worlds. The buttressing effect provided strength and there was space at the top of the end wall for a window as well (C). In many houses a double pitch was employed to provide more roof space, thus forming a gambrel or mansard roof (D).

As buildings became more complicated and spawned additions, the roofs had to follow suit, often producing awkward joins that invited rain to penetrate them and cause rot. Dormer windows were one source of trouble, the extensive roofs of double-pile houses a greater one. The earlier double piles and many of the larger houses of the period made use of numerous gables, and some had M-roofs (E). These had the great disadvantage of a central gutter, running from side to side, but it was at least better than the roofs of those double piles that had a central well in their roofs and the folly of an internal gutter to drain it. The only way to make these roofs watertight was by using large quantities of leadwork.

Thatch, tiles, slates
Roof coverings again depended on what was available locally. In the earlier Middle Ages, thatch of various kinds was universal, but tiles made of baked clay became increasingly common in the fourteenth and fifteenth centuries. They were less warm than a thatch roof, but this was hardly a consideration at a time when windows were unglazed; more importantly, tiles lasted far longer and were fireproof.

The tiles were laid on battens and held in place by oak pegs to stop them from slipping (F). Later these were replaced by 'nibs' and iron nails, which unfortunately were prone to rusting (G). The ridges and hips were finished by curved tiles which covered the angle. Occasionally these tiles were crested, but few remain outside museums (H).

Clay tiles were best hung on roofs with a pitch of about 50 to 60 degrees, and thatch was much the same. Slate was better on a lower pitch, 45 degrees or even 35 degrees, according to the kind of slate. This reduced the chances of the slates slipping without increasing the likelihood of the rain coming in. Many stones could be split to form tiles, and, although Welsh slates were already being shipped round the coast in small quantities, most slates found on inland English roofs before the arrival of the canals and, later, the railways, were of local origin.

Real slate was mostly confined to parts of the West Country and the north, apart from Scotland and Wales, but stone tiles were readily obtainable from the sandstone of the Weald and some of the Jurassic stones of the south and Midlands. Pennine stone again made good tiles, but it was heavy, and, given the low pitch of the roofs necessary to stop it slipping off, particularly strong framing was needed underneath, including a stout king-post rising up from a tie-beam to support a ridge-beam.

Gutters and downpipes
No longer were people content to let the rainwater simply run off the roofs of their houses, and it became common practice to put gutters along the eaves. They were made to slope gently downwards to a hopper or rainwater head, which funnelled the water into a downpipe.

Gutters were commonly made of wood, and since they filled with leaves and stagnant water, they soon rotted.

Lead was the ideal material for gutters, and leaden rainwater heads could be easily decorated (I and J). They became a good place for the house owner to inscribe his initials or some other symbol and the date; but the historian must remember that this is the date of the rainwater head and not necessarily the date of the house. The high price of lead, as well as its inclination to crack, eventually brought about its wholesale replacement with cast iron in the nineteenth century, and extensive theft more recently, with replacement in plastic. Both this and moulded fibreglass decay under the influence of ultra-violet light and last no better than traditional materials.

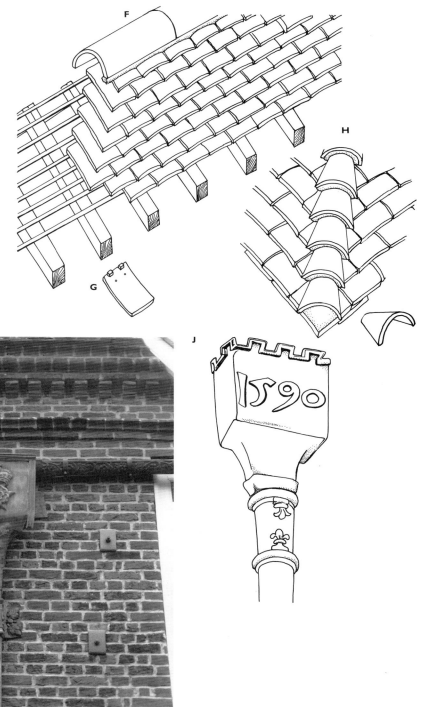

A

Chimney-stacks

With chimney-stacks revolutionizing the house between 1500 and about 1700 or so, they soon became an object of status. Consequently they might be built inordinately high or be highly decorated. This was true of houses large and small. Where yeoman houses were concerned, every locality developed characteristic types, especially where brick was used for their construction. This was because it was easier to cut or mould into decorative shapes, and it allowed several flues to be combined into one stack with greater ease than stone.

In Essex and East Anglia, the flues were often built within separate shafts to rise above the roof from a common base. These might be square and set diagonally, or they might be hexagonal or octagonal instead. Often their brickwork was decorated with cut or moulded patterns, and then finished with oversailing courses that linked the shafts together (A).

As time went by the oversailing courses became simpler (B), perhaps as bricklayers responded to Renaissance classicism, or the flues were combined into one stack which was decorated with angular ribs or panels suggesting individual shafts (C). To the south of London, where decoration was generally more severe, the shafts were plainer and relied more on over-sailing courses for their decoration (D and E).

By the middle of the seventeenth century, classical forms were beginning to prevail, and both brick and stone chimney-stacks were decorated with plain panels or arches beneath very plain tops where projecting courses of bricks or stone provided the only form of termination (F).

In those parts of the country where stone was hard but friable, for instance Cornwall and the Lake District, conical chimney-stacks were popular, if only because this was the most practical way of building them as soundly as possibe (G).

B

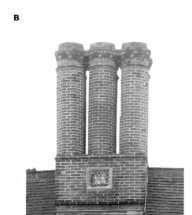

C

D

E

F

G

Privies

Most houses of this period still had outside privies close to the house, and these do not survive. They went by a number of euphemisms, the old French word *garderobe* being the earliest. House of office, necessary house and closet were later terms which shrouded this ticklish subject in an ever denser veil of modesty.

Just occasionally a house might have an internal privy, and, as of old, it might be no more than a small room (RIGHT). A bench with a hole in it was placed over a shute and this descended, perhaps alongside an external chimney-stack (BELOW), to ground level, where it emerged to discharge its contents where they would not, with as much luck as judgement, cause offence.

Fireplaces

Between them, enclosed fireplaces and glazed windows entirely changed the comfort inside a house. They did not, however, immediately change the appearance of the interior. Indeed this was to change only slowly through a process of evolution which took it almost imperceptibly from the medieval interior into something approaching today's.

The most obvious change was the enclosed hearth itself. The side and back of the fireplace were enclosed in brick or stone. Because these materials could calcify through exposure to the heat of the fire, it was customary in wealthy households to place an iron fireback (A) against them for protection. At a height of about 4 or 5 feet a timber beam or a stone lintel bridged the open front of the fireplace to carry the chimney-stack. This could be of timber, brick or stone, depending on the availability of local materials and the means to pay for them.

Chimney-stacks

Brick was the easiest material to use in the construction of a chimney-stack because several flues, for instance from back-to-back hearths on two storeys, could be combined into one stack without making it become excessively large and fill the interior of the house. For that reason, brick chimney-stacks sometimes appear in houses with stone walls.

On the other hand, timber was cheaper, and so it remained the standard material for stacks in the poorer parts of the country right into the eighteenth century (B). To make a timber chimney fireproof, the gaps between the timbers were filled with wattle and daub and well plastered. As often as not, these chimneys were set over ingles, where a family could draw up their chairs to sit when the nights were at their coldest.

The wood fires were encouraged to burn slowly and radiate a warm glow rather than to burn furiously, sending all the heat and a shower of sparks up the chimney, so timber chimneys

A

B

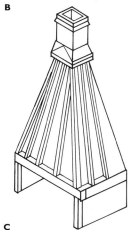

C

were not as impractical as they sound. Nevertheless, their comparative fragility has caused their universal destruction.

Chimney-pieces

Just as the chimney-stack itself was a source of pride and status exhibited to the outside world, so was the chimney-piece which surrounded the fireplace inside. Even if it comprised only a timber beam resting on a brick base, the beam or the whole surround could be carved or chamfered (c, page 103). The size alone of a stone lintel could be an object of status (D), as in a farmhouse at Chetnole, Dorset.

In the seventeenth century, fireplaces in parlours and the more formal rooms were increasingly framed with ornate surrounds. The stone or brick sides could be heavily moulded, and these mouldings could run without a break into a timber beam spanning them (E), even though a surround looked better if it stuck to one material (F, page 107). Nevertheless, the idea that

continued on page 107

Glencoyne is one of Cumbria's finest farmhouses. Dramatically sited overlooking Ullswater at Patterdale, it was built about 1629 from the hard local sandstone. This stone is so dark, and made all the darker by the lack of sunshine in the Lake District, that the house is whitewashed to distinguish it from the byre further down the slope. The roofs are covered in the abundant local slate, and more slates have been let into the window sills, the stepped gables and the bases of the chimneys to make sure that they too are properly waterproofed. The chimney-stacks are in the form of gently tapering cones, another characteristic local form.

Pennine houses are seldom whitewashed even though the carboniferous stones of the region are nearly as dark and hard as Cumbria's. The yeomen living in places like Sowerby on the hills to the west of Halifax were able to make a surprisingly good living from the later Middle Ages onwards by combining dairy farming and weaving, and the result is that the hills are dotted with many fine houses like Castle Farm (BELOW). Despite the hard stone there was money enough for a little carving, such as the decorative hood-moulds over the windows and the panel above the front door, bearing the initials and date 'INEN 1662'. The windows of this farmhouse are unusually grand in having two tiers of lights, set out in a stepped pattern in the upper storey, rather than long bands of individual lights in the local way.

One of the two bedrooms of Whitehouse Farm at Stannington (BELOW), looking out over the small stone-walled fields of the Pennines where oats and herds of cattle helped to make a living. The panel behind the bed is built up from a series of planks fitted into grooves cut into thicker studs, to provide an internal partition, a form of construction widely used in the west and north from the later Middle Ages until the eighteenth century.

continued from page 104

the surround consisted of two distinct parts, the sides and the top, remained. The emerging classical taste of the age reinforced this idea, and so the sides might be treated as piers or decorated with pilasters or columns, while the top was decorated with panels and even given a cornice that could act as an overshelf, above which there might be more decoration, reaching right to the ceiling on occasion (G and H). By and large the keystone was enough elaboration to make the fireplace the focus of the room even when it did not contain a hearty fire.

Just as the doorhead of the main entrance to a house or the base of its chimney-stack might be carved with the owner's initials and the date when it was built, the same was true for chimney-stacks. Occasionally the inscription might be more than the usual terse date and initials.

In Somerset, kitchen fireplaces sometimes were flanked by a chamber for smoking meat. Most of these have gone, but the sawn-off chimney-beam and the alcove to its right (I) show where a curing chamber used to exist.

F

G

H

I

Staircases

The enclosed hearth and chimney-stack made the continuous upper floor a reality in most houses. They therefore needed a staircase. Since the upper floor remained subsidiary for a long time, and sleeping upstairs was not universal until the eighteenth century, staircases generally received little attention at first. As houses became more spacious, this changed, and increasingly staircases became objects of status.

The treads and risers were made from separate planks of timber, and the stairs rose less steeply. Instead of being squeezed into corners, they were brought out into the open, for instance into the central vestibule of the later types of house. This was mainly achieved by allowing them to rise against a wall on one side and remain open on the other. Here they were given ornate timber balusters to support a carved handrail (A).

The balusters and rail of each flight terminated in a heavy post, a direct descendant of the newel posts which supported more tightly built stairways (B and C). These posts could be carved in various ways and might terminate, top and bottom, in an ornate pinnacle and pendant (D).

Balusters

The balusters might be flat or turned. Flat balusters were usually given fantastic shapes based on the most mannered forms of pilaster applied to grand houses, sometimes as mere templates, sometimes with their faces fully carved as well (E). The turned balusters were boldly cut into a number of stout forms, suggesting columns and capitals, or swelling in and out symmetrically about a central series of rings (F). Early handrails sometimes had a grip carved into the top, but more usually they were chamfered along the top edges or moulded along the sides (G).

A

B

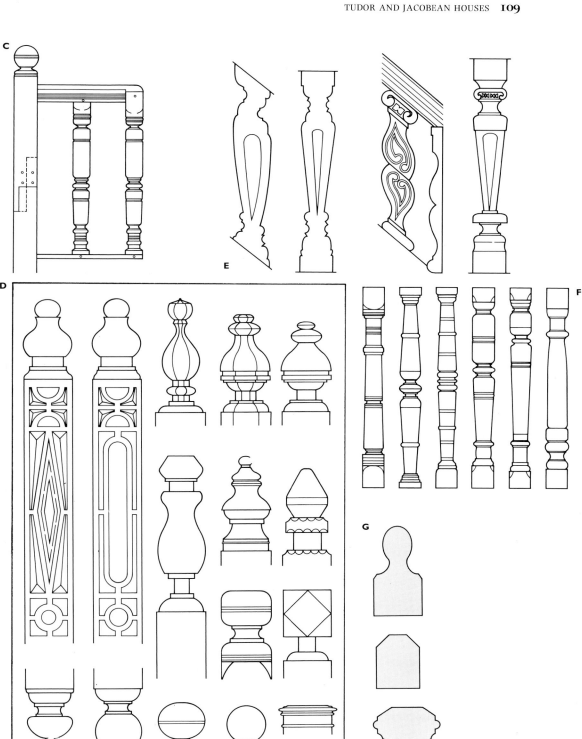

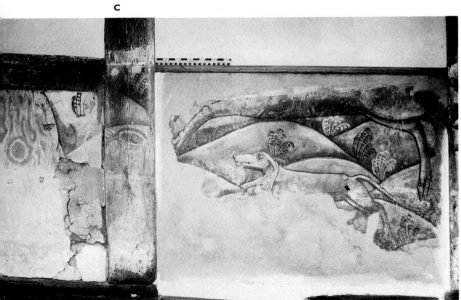

Walls

Whether the walls of a house were framed with timber and made of plastered wattle and daub, or built entirely of brick or stone, they were covered over. Either they were panelled, or plastered and painted or limewashed. They might also be covered over with painted cloths, a poor man's version of a tapestry. Otherwise both plastered and panelled walls might themselves be painted. Some internal walls might be no more than panelled partitions, as they had been in the Middle Ages.

The finish of the plainest walls was no more than it had been in the Middle Ages, simply a plaster coat on whatever material formed the wall. This might be colour-washed or painted with a number of patterns which often combined naturalistic and geometrical forms, and continued over plaster and timberwork alike (A), even when the design was divided into a series of panels. Other painted decorations might have a notional base, frieze or cornice (B), and occasionally might even provide a form of architectural surround to a door. Only rarely do scenes survive, such as this fragment of a hunting scene in which a wounded deer is leaping over a bloodthirsty hound in a house at Pinner in north London (C).

All surviving painting of these sorts is rare, and must have expert treatment if it is to be restored. It should always have some form of protection against the normal wear and tear to which walls are subjected.

Plasterwork

Decorated plasterwork started to come into its own in the sixteenth century, and developed beyond the pargetting of the Middle Ages with increasing finesse. Friezes of precast plaster emblems and naturalistic forms were sometimes used to decorate walls, and occasionally the ability to reproduce figures in quantity led to delightful absurdities, such as a frieze which shows Adam and Eve and the serpent in the apple tree in three different arrangements, over a fireplace in a house at Aldington in Kent (D).

Panelling

Panelled partitions were decorative in their own right if they were formed out of well cut planks set into chamfered or moulded studs. Panelling which was designed to hide the inside of a rough timber or brick wall needed no structural strength of its own, and so could be made from small panels set into a frame with mouldings scratched into its sides, or more properly cut into the tops and bottoms as well. Sometimes the panels were given a raised centre or carved into a linenfold pattern (E), although such carving was usually confined to grand houses.

Panelling of this kind was considered a fitting, not a fixture, and so, being prone to removal, was not generally designed to suit the dimensions of a specific room. This was not always the case, and panelling was sometimes fitted into an architectural scheme that more or less suited the shape of the room. This might be in the form of a frieze, or could embrace the space over a fireplace (F); and it might even include a series of panels which filled the spaces between ornate pilasters (G).

All in all, panelling allowed many different ornate forms which exactly suited the taste of the age for luxury, solidity and ornate forms. A whole house could be fully panelled to make up for the ornate roofs of medieval halls (H).

D

E

F

G

H

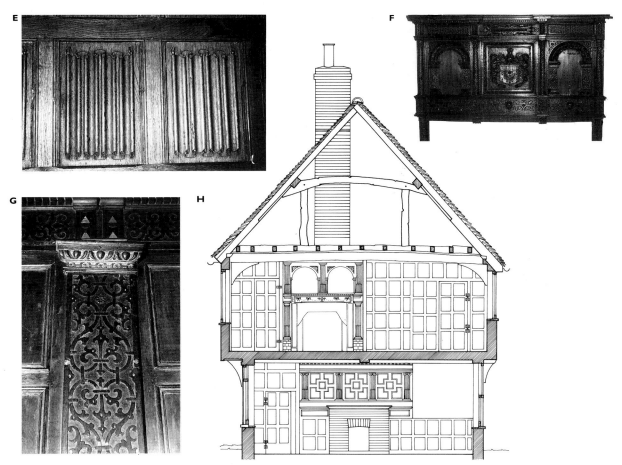

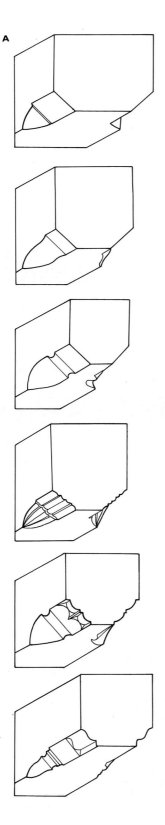

A

Ceilings

With the demise of the open hall and, with it, the status that was attached to its height and to the ornate timbering supporting the roof, attention turned to the undersides of the beams and joists that supported the floors overhead. At the very least, these could have their lower edges chamfered and the chamfers could be stopped in various ornate ways (A). The junction where beams joined each other might be the occasion to carve a badge (B), in the same way as the bosses of rib-vaulted churches had been carved in the Middle Ages where the ribs crossed over each other. Only in the most elaborate houses were the beams carved with anything more, such as twisting tendrils and foliage (C).

Patterns of this kind were more easily achieved when ceilings were battened and plastered. Then the forms of decoration applied to walls could also be applied here, and with the great advantage of their being less susceptible to damage. The designs might be no more than a few moulded symbols or figures arranged to form a pattern (D and E), but often they were set within intertwining lines or braids (F and G). Ideally these were formed into patterns which emphasized the centre and the edges of the ceiling as a kind of frame (H). This was the way that plastered ceilings would subsequently develop.

B

C

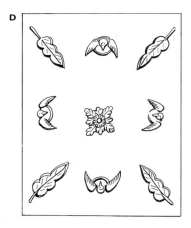

D

E

F

G

H

Georgian houses

The eighteenth century has been called the age of elegance, and indeed the imaginative use of serenely classical forms in the houses of this period says it all. There were to be no major advances in house planning beyond the achievements of the previous two centuries. Plans that were in existence soon after 1600 and had become widespread by 1700 remained the mainstay of the house builder. The one significant exception was the design of the terrace, and even here a standard plan had been evolved well before George I came to the throne in 1714.

His accession brought the Whigs political power. They promoted a change in architectural taste that turned its back on the distinctive baroque style of Sir Christopher Wren and his associates, Nicholas Hawksmoor and Sir John Vanbrugh. In its place came the revived classicism of the devotees of the Italian Renaissance architect, Andrea Palladio, and his English follower Inigo Jones, with Lord Burlington and the Scottish architect Colen Campbell at their head.

None of these new men was involved in building houses for common people, but their influence on taste and consequently on the style of everyday houses was overwhelming. The vigorous style of the seventeenth century, in which medieval and Renaissance motifs came together in a bravura display of self-confidence, gave way to chastely correct classical forms. Occasionally, there was a playful Gothic touch that had no more to do with the Middle Ages than its courtly romantic inventors had to do with the clerical lords who had been the principal builders three hundred years beforehand.

However correctly the gentlemen of the eighteenth century pursued the classical ideal, there were marked changes in taste in the Georgian period, and these were fully reflected in house design. While Georgian England properly began with the accession of the first of the Hanoverians in 1714, and continued to the death of George IV's brother William IV in 1837, politically it was founded well before that with the 'Glorious Revolution' and the accession of William and Mary in 1689; and artistically its origins lay even earlier in the work of Inigo Jones. So long a period could hardly be without changes in taste and style.

Industrial and urban development
Developments in taste fade into insignificance as society itself changed through the consequences of the Industrial Revolution and an unprecedented growth in population. How this affected the way people lived was, for many, anything but beautiful and elegant, and it, too, showed in the houses of the period.

At the start of the eighteenth century the population stood at rather less than six million. By 1837, the population had more than doubled to well over twelve million, and was increasing at an extraordinary rate. No longer was a minority of this population living in towns; nor were the towns the same. The old market towns that had been founded in the Middle Ages were either growing to inordinate size under the stimulus of industries which had been revolutionized by the factory system, or were bowing to new industrial towns that had been no more than villages a few decades beforehand.

The whole emphasis of house building consequently changed. The new demand was for houses in town. Only the enclosure of once open fields to make new farms provided a great impetus to build new houses in the countryside. The attraction of many towns was so great that houses were fitted into every open space in the centre to accommodate a new industrial class. But for many people, paradoxically probably a declining proportion of the total population, there was money to be made, and this urban middle class looked to the healthier fringes of town for a place to live.

If the exuberance of the architectural styles of the sixteenth and seventeenth centuries reflects the bucolic confidence of yeomen and merchants who knew what they liked, the restrained classicism of the eighteenth and early nineteenth centuries reflects the gentility of an age that liked good manners and respected correct behaviour. The division between taste and the drudgery which supported it became more marked as the years passed, and this, too, is visible in the houses of the age.

Partly through tradition, partly through the greater mobility of urban life, even rich people seldom purchased a house in town, let alone a new house. Instead they leased one, completing the last link in a long chain of landlord, speculator and craftsman-builder who, between them, had organized its construction and physically built it.

The old days when country yeomen built for themselves and their descendants were largely over. Instead of people pleasing themselves in this way and mixing fashion and tradition in what they chose, they now chose from ready-made houses. These appealed to taste by keeping up with every whim of fashion, but, being inexpensive, they also appealed to the speculators who financed them, and so they were built to proved stock patterns, in both planning and decoration, because these would find a ready market. Fashion itself was promoted by an ever-increasing list of pattern books.

The terrace house

These are the reasons why the terrace house was so successful. It could be built in large numbers, even though by a process that seems to have been chaotically managed because so many people were involved in its construction and financing. In practice, the terrace house was anything but chaotic. It imposed regularity on a street where there might otherwise have been the chaos of individual, disordered building. So each terrace was more than the sum of its individual houses, and standardized ornament enhanced these qualities. The terrace exemplified the sense of order inherent in the classical taste that then held sway, and its restrained decoration demonstrated the same taste through ornate door surrounds, fine chimney-pieces, rich plaster ceiling cornices, carved and turned staircase balusters, and all kinds of ornaments which added status without excessive cost.

As the eighteenth century progressed, this ornament increasingly became the subject of influential pattern books, many of them written by the leading architects of the day. They, the experts, publicized a great variety of classical forms, and showed how they could be applied to doorways, chimney-pieces and indeed all kinds of decorative features which introduced builders and the public alike to what would most fashionably adorn their houses. All the while the keynote was taste and order.

The terrace itself imposed another kind of order. It was increasingly built to a number of patterns described in the books, and in a number of standard sizes. Usually there would be one size in one street, another in another, so that there were good streets and less good streets. This was a clear reflection of the desire for greater physical divisions between the classes of society. These divisions were even reflected within the house itself, so far as the ground-floor and first-floor rooms were the most important and were the abode of the master and his immediate family, while the basement and attics were the least important and occupied by servants. No longer were servants members of an economic unit as they had been in the countryside. They usually played no part in the master's profession or trade, and so became a lesser breed, with divisions even among themselves that separated cook from skivvy.

On the outside of the house, these divisions were reflected in the size of the windows. The basement windows were small, and sometimes hardly visible, so low were they set. The windows above were large and clearly visible, but the uppermost windows would again be smaller as befitted classical ideas of proportion and the lowly status of the rooms they served; the top windows might even be hidden behind a parapet, an apt symbol for the scant regard shown to the lowlier servants.

Materials and decoration

Depending on the resources of the locality, houses were now generally made of brick or stone. These had more status than timber, and anyway were often cheaper. Where timber was still the major building material, houses were often tile-hung or plastered. Specially shaped tiles known as mathematical tiles gave a passable imitation of brick, and plaster could be grooved or channelled to look like masonry.

Before the eighteenth century was out, the taste for the picturesque on occasion oddly reversed these fashions, and brought the first *cottages ornées*, houses pretending to be the rustic cottages of the past, replete with timbering and thatch. In the Georgian period, these houses had a frivolous quality, but they were to lead to a more serious style in the Victorian period that would last to the present.

The main decorative feature of the outside of each house was its doorway. Doorways had always needed some form of emphasis, and, in a long terrace, each door needed even more of this, simply to indicate the individual houses. Up until the early part of the eighteenth century, front doors were usually emphasized by hoods supported by ornately carved brackets. These served to keep the rain off the doorway, in the way that grander houses could rely on projecting porches. By the middle of the century, fashion rather than practicality dispensed with projecting hoods and instead required some form of classical entablature or even a pediment supported on a pair of pilasters or half columns, placed one each side of the door. These were usually made of wood, but the need to avoid combustible material and, once again, the working of fashion brought stucco into prominence later.

One of the most remarkable decorative features of the later eighteenth century was the use of a form of fired pottery called Coade stone after its manufacturer and designer, Eleanor Coade. She, uniquely, represented women in the male-dominated world of building. Her stoneware was used for all kinds of architectural decoration, none more characteristic than the keystones with moulded heads on them which appear ubiquitously in houses of the period.

Doors were now more elaborate. Apart from the cheap plank doors to servants' quarters, they were made from a frame of vertical and horizontal timbers called styles and rails; these were grooved to take panels, usually a pair at the top, another pair in the middle and a further pair at the bottom, though there were many variations.

In front of the house, wooden posts gave way to wrought-iron railings as the eighteenth century drew on, and these in turn gave way to cheaper cast iron, which allowed fashionable designs to be mass-produced in large numbers to meet an insatiable demand for decorative railings, lamp-holders, balconies and even porches.

Well before the end of the seventeenth century the sash window was taking the place of the casement. It consisted of a pair of sliding frames or sashes set in pairs of vertical grooves, an outer sash above and an inner sash below, to make the window weathertight. Only the upper one of these double sashes opened at first, and it had to be propped open, but soon both sashes could slide open and shut, and they were counterbalanced by weights hung from them on ropes running over pulleys. At the start of the eighteenth century, the boxes which contained the counterweights were set flush with the outer face of the window. Towards the end of the eighteenth century, largely through a greater desire to reduce the amount of visible woodwork, the sash boxes were rebated into the inner face of the wall and so became almost invisible from the outside.

The sash window was taller than it was wide, and its proportions were carefully graded to fit into the front of a house. The need to maintain the ordering of an elevation meant that sometimes a window was needed on the outside where there was no room for it inside, so a blank panel was put in its place. Windows were taxed from 1696 to 1851, and this has led to the idea that many of these blind windows were an attempt to avoid the tax, but it is rarely the case.

In the countryside some houses were too low for tall windows, and horizontal bands of windows continued in use, with opening casements set among them. A few houses were given horizontally sliding sashes, sometimes called Yorkshire sliding sashes, although they were not confined to that county, or even to the north.

At the start of the eighteenth century, the roof line of most fashionable houses was marked by an elaborate wooden cornice, set under the eaves. It might be moulded but was often carved with rich classical decoration, even though the houses lacked classical columns or pilasters on their front elevations. These eaves cornices were a fire hazard as the flames could easily catch them and spread to a neighbouring house. In the City of London they were outlawed in 1707, and parapets were put in their place. Elsewhere it is debatable whether it was the risk of fire or attention to fashion that made the parapet popular, but, since parapets made it harder for rain to run off a roof, it is likely that fashion had most to do with their popularity.

Extensive guttering was now applied to the eaves of most houses to lead rainwater well away from the walls. Ornamental hoppers or rainwater heads made of lead became a prominent feature of many houses, and even the downfall pipe and its spout might be ornamented. By the end of the eighteenth century these were more usually made of iron and their decoration fell out of fashion until the Victorians revived it.

Interior style

Inside houses, the boarded floor became universal for all except the servants' workrooms, which generally had flagged stone floors. Very lavish houses might have decorative floors laid with stone or tiles set in geometric patterns. The stairs sometimes had stone treads, which were cantilevered from the wall that supported one side of the staircase.

Inside most houses, timber retained its usefulness for longer than it did outside. It was now seldom indigenous oak but imported fir shipped from the Baltic, and, in the nineteenth century, pine was coming from Canada as well. Wood panelling remained a common way of finishing walls, though the panels became much larger, and usually comprised a single panel stretching from the skirting up to about waist height to form a dado, and a second panel above that stretching up to a cornice. The panels were well proportioned, just as sash windows were, and set in moulded frames. As the eighteenth century progressed, the upper panels were omitted and the walls were plastered instead. They might be painted with tinted water-based paint, or they might be covered in patterned wallpaper, although this was expensive and, adding to its cost, was taxed. Eventually the lower panel was abandoned too, except where it might protect a wall from scuffing, such as in a passage or up a staircase.

The cornice between wall and ceiling was an occasion for decoration even in the plainest of rooms. It might be no more than a moulding run out by the plasterer, but it could be set with preformed ornament of various classical types, and might even be integrated into a scheme of plastering that embraced both the walls and the ceiling, and emphasized doorways and window openings.

The windows on all but the top floors still had shutters, both for security and privacy. Increasingly shutters were made in two sets of folding leaves that could be housed in boxes each side of the window, and then gave the appearance of small panels angled to the window which diffused the light around the room. Occasionally shutters were arranged as rising sashes installed in a box at the base of the frame. It was in the later nineteenth century that fabric curtains took their place.

During the seventeenth century, sea coal brought through local ports from collieries around the Tyne, the Severn and other rivers became the main fuel to keep town fires burning. Coal, unlike wood, does not benefit from burning slowly on a great heap of embers, and, since it burns at a higher temperature than wood, smaller fires were adequate. To provide a good draught, the fires were made in small iron grates, set into fireplaces seldom more than about 2 feet square. They were raised above an ash pit, and often fitted with hobs where kettles could be boiled for making pots of expensive but fashionable tea, and where small pans could heat snacks. These grates provided an opportunity for various decorative effects, contrasting with the surrounding chimney-piece, which might take the form of a tiled, fireproof surround set within a classical architrave, with a mantel shelf that gave them the common name of mantelpiece.

Since a fire was the centre of a room as well as a symbol of hospitality, it prompted the most decoration, and was always designed for show. In the cheapest of houses, there might be a plain wooden or stone surround, and only taste limited the ostentation that wealth could bring to a chimney-piece in a rich salon. The whole gamut of classical ornament was applied to their decoration, and this was augmented by carved panels on the chimney-piece itself and elaborate over-mantels with mirrors and much carving that extended right up to the ceiling.

Staircases became more elaborate so far as the individual treads extended slightly beyond the string that carried them, and this consequently had to be cut into the shape of the individual steps. These so-called open strings accentuated the tread ends, and they were often decorated with a scroll to highlight them even further. The treads themselves, rather than the string, carried turned balusters with elegantly refined curves or with barley-sugar twists. By the end of the century, such ornament was thought to be excessive and, increasingly, balusters were made of thin rectangular strips of wood that seemed to be hardly strong enough to support their elegantly curving rails.

With so much decoration, it was a simple matter to differentiate between the master's and family's quarters and the servants'. The stairs down to the basement and up to the attic would still have closed strings, while the main stairs had ornate open strings. The doors in the basement might still be no more than plank doors with latches, while the best doors were panelled and had mortised locks and elegant china handles. Upstairs there might be simpler and thinner panelled doors with their locks not mortised but attached to the face of the frame, and made of brass in the main rooms or iron in the lesser ones. The handles would possibly be of brass rather than china. In the attics there might be plainer doors still, perhaps with no more than latches. The attic rooms devoted to the most junior servants, such as the general servant or maid, would have no fire at all, while the most senior servant, such as the cook or butler, would have a small fire, but with a plain surround. Gradations of status were everywhere to be seen. There was a place for everyone, and everyone knew his place.

A

B

C

D

Detached houses

Although there were no significant new plans for houses developed during the later seventeenth and eighteenth centuries, the appearance of houses varied extensively among already established types and as changes in style took effect. Tradition dies hard, and the styles of the seventeenth century lasted well into the eighteenth, especially in places beyond the influence of London and a few other important centres of fashion.

Provincial building

In the countryside this was especially the case whenever a house was built independently from the taste of a great landed estate. It could easily assume a style that was at least fifty years behind the latest fashions of the day. This is evident in an attractive farmhouse at Cobham in Kent (A), which was given a new front in 1712 and a plaque to record it. Cobham is not far from London, but, where style goes, it could have been built some thirty years before its date. Its plan was not at all new either, and takes the form of symmetrically disposed rooms each side of a lobby entry. In fact, the old lobby-entry plan continued for a long while into the eighteenth century for small houses, if only because it could easily be built in a fashionably symmetrical form.

Despite the longevity of the lobby-entry plan, especially among poorer houses that were still made from timber, the more useful plan with a central entrance vestibule and chimney-stacks on the end walls remained standard for smaller houses. It was particularly useful in villages where houses abutted each other or their farm buildings.

There were many ways of increasing the accommodation of these houses. One was to extend the rear service room into a fully fledged extension for a kitchen, scullery and wash-house. Another way was simply to extend the frontage as in an unusually grand farmhouse built on the granite of West Penwith in 1721 at Paul,

Cornwall (B). Right at the other end of the scale, a minimal variant of the plan was used for lowly wayside cottages in which the entrance opened straight into the living room and the staircase rose directly from it to bedrooms in what were, at most, lofts (C).

Urban influences

Now that towns were growing apace, they were in the vanguard of building. Fashion travelled from them to the countryside, not vice versa. This led to the appearance of a number of remarkably tall farmhouses, although they had the inconvenience of a second and even a third staircase to reach their top storeys. When they stand alone, like a farmhouse at Calverton in Nottinghamshire (D), they have an oddly urban appearance. They look more at home among the tightly packed houses of Midlands villages, where

farmhouses often took on an L-shaped plan, at once to shelter their farmyards and to make the best use of restricted sites.

In several parts of the north and the west, upper storeys were particularly favoured because they provided ideal accommodation for spinning and weaving wool. On the Pennines, between Halifax and Manchester, dozens of farmhouses were given new top storeys to house looms as yeoman farmers in the later eighteenth century augmented their incomes with the profits from weaving. They are immediately distinguishable by their long bands of windows, which provided essential illumination for the looms. At Diggle, high on the edge of Saddleworth Moor, a farmhouse was given a new, raised upper storey in the middle of the eighteenth century, and, about fifty years later, it was joined by a

purpose-built house with long bands of windows on all of its three storeys (E).

Double-pile plan

The double pile remained the most economic plan where building materials were concerned, so it was often built by landowners when they invested money in improving their estates. This type of house attracted good tenants, since they could reserve the front rooms for their own use, with the rear ones for their servants and the farmhands. Simultaneously, it attracted landowners because they knew that they could build a large house at the least cost. So popular was this type of house that it continued its life as the villa of the leafier suburbs of growing towns (F), where it brought the romantic aura of the countryside to the fringes of their increasingly squalid centres.

Just occasionally a house was built that had all the appearance of a large villa, or conversely of a short terrace, but was in fact a pair of semi-detached houses. There is an early eighteenth-century pair close to Greenwich Park in south-east London, and another pair, nearby at Blackheath (G), which were built in 1776, still a notably early date. It was only in the nineteenth century that the semi-detached house became popular, and in the 1920s and 1930s that it took over from the terrace as the firm favourite among speculative builders.

E

F

G

Terrace houses

Although the terrace was an old concept, it was not until the architect Inigo Jones was commissioned to design the principal buildings on the Earl of Bedford's Covent Garden estate in the 1630s that the terrace house began its long, fashionable carreer in earnest. The order that Jones imported from Palladian Italy to Charles I's London even then had to wait for the end of the Civil War and the Commonwealth that followed before it was widely used again. In fact it was the impetus for rebuilding after the Great Fire in 1666 that made all the difference. The Act for Rebuilding of 1667 emphasized the sense of order inherent in the terrace, and, in the hands of speculators like the notorious Nicholas Barbon, who also initiated fire insurance for buildings, it was set on its course.

Early plans

For a generation after the Great Fire, terrace houses were still built with their staircases placed between the front and back rooms. In the houses of Bloomsbury Square, built about 1664, the space behind the staircase between the two main rooms was used as a closet where food for snacks could be kept, china and cutlery could be stored, clothes hung, or chamber pots hidden away until the servants came to empty them (A). There was some structural sense in this arrangement as the stairs could be easily supported, but little more than that. The stairs were hard to illuminate, and needed either a light-well or some form of lantern in the roof. Neither of these was particularly satisfactory.

By about 1700, a solution was devised. The staircase was removed to one side of the rear, to rise from the end of the passage leading back from the main entrance, and to turn rather more than half way up at a small landing, built against the back wall and illuminated by a window (B). The main difficulty with this arrangement was that in a small house closets either became little more than poky cupboards, or they had to be built as small extensions projecting from the back wall, as they are here in a house built on Sir James Smith's estate in Westminster over sixty years later than the house in Bloomsbury Square. The placing of closets apart, the plan easily catered for everyone's needs, and served houses large and small thereafter. Size and style were to be the main differentiating features between them.

Elevations

The style of a terrace house was mainly expressed in its front elevation. In the middle of the seventeenth century, terraces took their cue from Inigo Jones's houses at Covent Garden, and so they incorporated pilasters into their design to articulate the two main storeys above the ground floor.

This is evident in a remarkable survivor from 1658, the terrace of four houses facing Newington Green in Islington (c, page 125), shown here as they probably were before unsightly shops were built into their ground floors, and other changes made. There are many old-fashioned features about their design, such as their plan and the gables, which sit rather more uneasily above the pilasters than a classical parapet would do. The window frames are again of the old type, with mullions and transoms dividing them like a cross, and the windows themselves have opening casements.

Despite all that, the pilasters are not mere decoration, but serve to articulate the façade, first by dividing it into classically proportioned bays and, secondly, by grouping the windows of the main storeys together, leaving the attic windows of the servants' rooms demonstrably separate in the old-fashioned gables. Even these windows do better than the windows of the kitchens and sculleries in the basement where the servants worked.

For the next two centuries and more, pilasters and even attached columns would continue to

continued on page 125

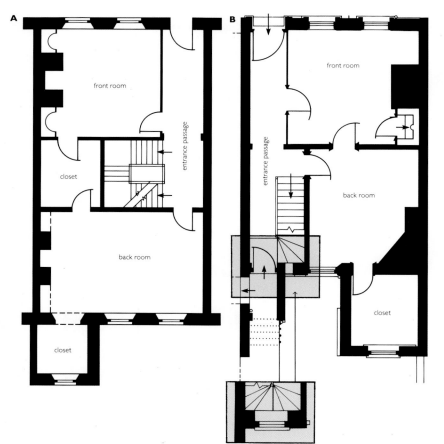

Looke Farm at Puncknowle,
Dorset, has the symmetry and
classical detailing of the
eighteenth century but treated in
so naïve a fashion that it seems
that its mason was unfamiliar
with it. Only when he came to the

huge ears of wheat supporting the
urn over the blind 'fanlight' above
the entrance does he appear to
have felt completely at home. The
house was built as early as 1700
when not all masons could
practise the new style fluently.

But this house is odder still because
the fireplaces and consequently
the chimney-stacks are in the
corners of the house, suggesting
an upturned cabinet with its legs
in the air.

The classical style took time to spread northwards across the country and downwards through society. Though only regular spacing and the architraves round the windows and main doorway of Hall Farm at Newbiggin, Cumbria (BELOW), show the arriving classical style, this farmhouse was built as early as 1695 and, moreover, in the far north. At that time, manorial landlords like those who built this house were still building less fashionable farmhouses for their tenants in the more up-to-date south.

The Bailiff's House at Park Farm, Shugborough, Staffordshire (BELOW), is a typical late Georgian farmhouse, with symmetrical, widely spaced sash windows, a central door and fanlight set in a correctly detailed Doric portico, and a low-pitched roof. The Palladian wings of the house reinforce the classical effect and only the functionally placed chimney-stacks upset the overall symmetry. The house was designed about 1800 for the first Viscount Anson by an expert, Samuel Wyatt, the most successful farm architect of his time.

continued from page 122

articulate the façades of terrace houses in the same way, but builders soon learned how to do without them, implying their proportions in other ways. Fifty years later than the Newington Green houses, the bricklayer and speculative builder Thomas Lucas built a street of terrace houses in Deptford (D), and these were up to date in their planning. They had staircases built against their back walls with windows to illuminate half landings and small projecting closets.

The fronts no longer had columns or pilasters for articulation, but instead were divided into a series of well-proportioned inset panels which articulate both the bays into which the windows and entrances fit, and the storeys between them. The blank panels above the entrances are not where windows were blocked to avoid the window tax, but a continuation of the pattern.

This pattern continues right up to the parapet, a novel feature, since the walls of most houses at this time met the roof with overhanging eaves. Here the parapet continues above the base of the roof so there has to be a gutter behind it. It also obscures the dormer windows of the attic. They are not shown in the drawing, nor were they meant to be seen. The attic rooms belonged to the servants, so their windows were not allowed too much

C

D

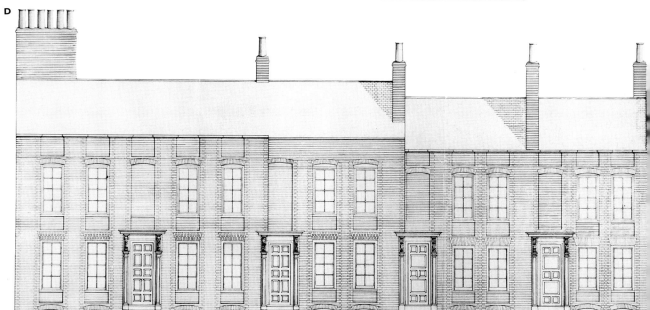

prominence and the parapet admirably kept them out of sight from the street.

Contemporary with Lucas's houses in Deptford are the earliest houses in Queen Square, Bristol (E). They make an interesting comparison. Instead of inset panels, here the houses are articulated by stucco quoining between them, bands of projecting brickwork between the storeys, and a boldly carved classical cornice beneath the eaves.

The house on Sir James Smith's Westminster estate (F) came twenty years later still, and is generally similar to Lucas's houses, but it lacks their panels and its front elevation relies for its proportions on the shape and position of the windows themselves. They articulate the front almost alone, although there is a band comprising three raised courses of brickwork to differentiate the storeys. In this case the ground storey was

stuccoed at a later date, probably in the early years of the nineteenth century, to bring it into line with later taste.

Building legislation

In 1774 Parliament at last passed an effective Building Act which regulated standards of construction so that jerry-building could be stamped out and houses simultaneously be made more fireproof. To achieve this, a number of standards were set. These included a detailed definition of four 'rates' of houses, each depending on their size, height, number of storeys, floor area, value and so on, and, for each, detailed requirements for wall thicknesses and joist sizes, and certain precautions against fire were made mandatory. Penalties included the demolition of any building which contravened the new building regulations.

As a guide, some of the flood of

copybooks which had guided builders already for half a century were now devoted to explaining the rates. There was a need for this since the Building Act seemed to be clear enough, but the definitions of the rates were full of contradictions. Nevertheless, the four rates that applied to terrace houses gained so much authority that houses could be advertised as First Rate, Second Rate, Third Rate and Fourth Rate, and everybody knew what this meant.

While the rates were differentiated by size, they shared the more restrained ornament of the last quarter of the eighteenth century, a restraint that lasted until the 1830s. For the sake of reducing combustibility, wooden decoration, in the form of cornices and door surrounds, and even the window frames were banished from sight, to be replaced by stucco and ironwork. For nearly half a century, fashion lingered with the forms of correct

E

F

classicism that architects such as the Adam brothers, James Stuart and Nicholas Revett, and Sir William Chambers had seen and drawn for themselves at classical sites around the Mediterranean, and now made available to all through their publications.

The four rates

The rates of house are not always easy to identify in practice, but generally large houses with four full storeys above a basement and a width great enough to allow three windows across their fronts belong to the first rate. This first-rate house in St Marylebone (G)

has its ground storey stuccoed and a stucco cornice and parapet to complete the elevation. The second-rate houses in Cross Street, Islington (H) have three windows across their fronts, but only three main storeys above their basements. The attic is set within the roof and has dormer windows for light.

The third-rate houses in Stonesfield Street (I) were built much later with only two windows on each floor. As the houses were narrower, it was impossible to align the upper windows with the entrance door and window of the ground floor

because the windows had to be placed symmetrically in their rooms and the door had to align with the entrance passage. The round heads of the windows of the ground floor and the blind arches over the windows of the upper storey were one of the main features of houses built from just before the start of the French Wars in 1793 until well after Waterloo in 1815.

Finally, a short row in Liverpool Road (J) of some of the few remaining fourth-rate houses are different in their small size with only two storeys above the basement.

G

H

I

J

Town houses and villas

The Building Acts only applied to central London, because it was by far the largest city in the kingdom with the most pressing problems and so Parliament acted to solve them. Elsewhere the Building Acts had an effect only because they were bound up with changes in fashion, and builders looked to London in matters of style.

Just before the start of the eighteenth century, cross-shaped mullions and transoms were still how most windows were framed, and most houses still had wooden eaves cornices, both visible in the former Lewisham Vicarage in south-east London (A). Sash windows and rather more verticality in the proportions marked the houses of the early part of the new century, as a house facing Stepney Green (B) shows clearly. The London Building Acts of 1707 and 1709 forbade both timber cornices and windows set in frames flush with the wall face as they were fire hazards, and, although the Acts did not apply elsewhere, the parapets and recessed windows that they brought about became widespread fashions, for instance in a house of 1718 at Thaxted in Essex (C).

By the second half of the eighteenth century a new fashion for Gothic made its first popular appearance as a playful alternative to classical, for instance in the so-called Speedwell Castle at Brewood in Staffordshire (D). All the same, the classical style remained a firm favourite and developed from the Italianate style of a villa on Richmond Hill (E), built in 1775, to the neo-Greek of another villa, built early in the nineteenth century in Bathwick Hill, Bath (F).

The popularity of the villa did not leave the terrace unaffected. Several streets of houses were built as though they were linked semi-detached pairs, as in a terrace at Blackheath of about 1835 (G), or completely semi-detached at New Cross (H).

E

F

G

H

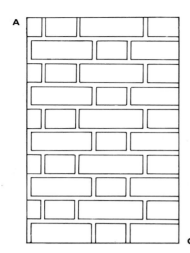

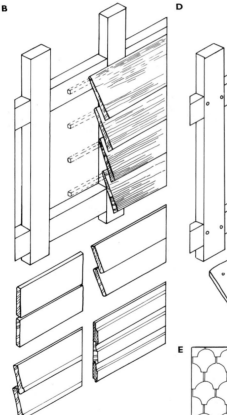

Building materials

By the eighteenth century, brick and stone reigned supreme as building materials, although that did not mean that they were used universally. Bricks were now generally laid with headers and stretchers alternating in each course, and with a header laid above a stretcher in the course below, a method known as Flemish bond (A).

Bricks

As fashion changed in London, the red-brown bricks of the earlier part of the eighteenth century gave way to yellow-grey bricks. They were thought to be closer to the colour of stone and therefore more acceptable, since stone was held in higher esteem than brick. The fine brighter red bricks used for quoins, arches and surrounds also fell out of fashion to be superseded by fine yellow bricks.

Outside London, local traditions withstood innovation, but during the last part of the century brick travelled quite widely by canal, and the railways helped this even further after 1840. Even in the 1830s greyish white Suffolk gaults were being used in London, where the market for bricks was insatiable.

Stucco and weather-boarding

By the later part of the eighteenth century, brickwork was often covered over with various patent cements, which generally went by the name of stucco. Stucco was often lined-out or channelled to look like courses of masonry and, at first, left in its natural grey-brown colour, in emulation of stone, but, as dirt clung to it and gave it a drab appearance, it was at first painted and even grained to look like stone, and later simply painted white or cream or some other light colour.

Timber-framed houses were altered again, in the name of fashion this time, rather than modernization. Horizontal weather-boarding (B) gave them a new appearance and removed the frame from view together with its connotations of age. The boards were usually made to overlap to make them weatherproof. On occasion, for instance in The Pantiles at Tunbridge Wells in Kent (c), the boarding was laid flat instead, and rebated with horizontal grooves suggesting the appearance of stucco trying to look like stone, a complicated deception which deceives no one. Meanwhile pargetted houses could also be lined out so that their plaster coat looked like individual blocks of masonry.

Hanging tiles

More commonly the frame was hung with tiles (D), a good way of reproducing the colour of brickwork, though not its appearance. The tiles made a good weatherproof exterior, but the iron nails that fixed the tiles to the battens could eventually rust, breaking the holes in the tiles and causing them to fall away. The lower ends of the tiles could be shaped so that a number of patterns resulted, both on a roof or on a tile-hung wall (E and F).

One way of shaping tiles, widely used in the south-east, was the most deceptive of all the devices for changing the appearance of a house. So-called mathematical tiles were shaped with a step so that the tiles could overlap in such a way that they looked like bricks (G). The corners could produce problems, often solved by attaching wooden borders or quoining.

Roof tiles

Roof tiles were more varied than before, and, in the early years of the eighteenth century, some eastern counties took to pantiles (H), an ancient form imported in the later seventeenth century before home production began. Pantiles were double curved and this allowed neighbouring horizontal tiles to overlap. This greatly reduced the likelihood of water penetration and so the overlap between the tiles up and down could be reduced to a minimum. The pitch of the roof could then be reduced below the 50 degrees normally used for standard tiles, lightening the overall weight, and so allowing a lighter timber structure.

Modern cement tiles are a poor replacement for pantiles, lacking both their shape and texture. Indeed few other replacements for traditional roof covering are so deadening in effect unless it is the habit of covering old slate roofs with fabric and a rubber compound. This not only ruins the appearance of the roof, but also makes an airtight seal, trapping moisture inside the roof as well as keeping rain out. There is no surer way of making a new roof inevitable.

Wood

Oak was becoming increasingly expensive, and roofs were more commonly being made from imported fir from the Baltic. It was less strong than oak, size for size, and so a light roof covering, such as pantiles, was beneficial.

Nearly all the parts of the house which formerly had been made of oak were now made of fir, pine or other kinds of soft wood. This included structural timbers, such as roof joists and floor beams, and also partitions, panelling, doors and carved decoration. Some of the more expensive woods, especially those with an attractive grain, were left in their natural state.

When soft woods were used on the exterior, they were always painted, both to improve their appearance and to preserve them. They were usually painted when used inside as well, again to improve their appearance. The modern craze for stripped pine is not a reflection of eighteenth-century taste.

F

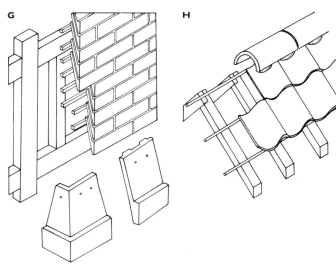

G

H

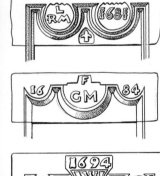

Doorways

The attractions of both fashion and tradition, and the advances of fashion itself, brought great variety to the elevations of Georgian houses, and in particular to their entrance doorways. Style meant one thing in London, another high on the Pennines, as it always had done.

Door hoods

Around 1700, entrances were commonly protected by hoods. They were usually supported by brackets, which could be in the form of classical scrolls, often heavily enriched with swags of flowers and fruit (A), or putti (B). All these were heavily encrusted with paint until recent stripping and repainting. The carved porches of the houses in Queen Anne's Gate, Westminster, took ornament to an extreme of luxuriance (c). The porches were usually flat, but rounded ones with a shell set inside them (D), or, later, a fanlight, were a popular alternative.

Door cases

Increasingly, builders brought classical elements into the design of their doorcases, sometimes to the disadvantage of the hood. In 1699 a fine brick classical pediment was added to a cottage in Berstead, West Sussex, but however much fashion it brought, it added no protection against the pouring rain (E).

Practicality and the advancing taste for classical forms were not always pulling in opposite directions. But the absurdities of a preference for taste rather than practicality are clearly demonstrated by adjacent houses in Great James Street, Holborn, where a sensible hood supported by ornate brackets has been replaced by a classical door surround complete with attached half columns, entablature and pediment (F). Indeed there is a double absurdity here, for not only does the classical surround offer far less shelter, but it takes its form from the temples of classical antiquity in which these pedimented fronts were designed as porches specifically to act as shelters from the weather.

There was a similar preoccupation with fashion far away on the Pennines. Here the protection given by a porch might seem to be essential, but perhaps the weather is so bad that no one thought them worthwhile. If you are going to get wet, you are going to get wet. At all events, the Pennines went their own way with classical forms making only a desultory appearance. At the start of the eighteenth century, looping patterns were all the rage in the Dales (G), and some of these still had a Gothic flavour (H), but they were slowly repressed by straighter lines and, eventually, classical cornices and pediments of sorts (I).

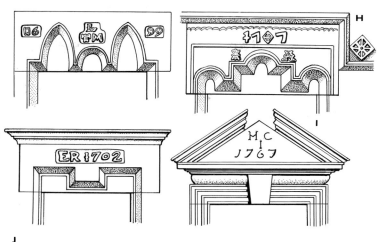

Fanlights

The window set above the entrance to light the passage or vestibule that led from it to the staircase at the rear gave the doorway a whole new form of decoration. Fanlights were given more and more decorative leadwork, and sometimes were left without hoods over them so that they would not be obscured. This development went hand in hand with the removal of wooden doorcases and porches to avoid the risk of fire spreading from one house to another, and the introduction of stucco decoration in their place.

Fanlights were first introduced into houses with projecting porches, and, when these had a pediment, the base was opened to let in the light (J). By the 1780s, wooden porches had given way to stucco or Coade stone surrounds, leaving the decoratively patterned fanlights to speak for themselves, as, for instance, they do at Bedford Square, Holborn (K). Their semicircular shape gave great scope for radiating patterns, plain and fancy. Fanlights were often rectangular, but this did not mean that they were much less ornate than semi circular ones (L).

With these ornamental surrounds came the new form of framed door, often with their panels emphasized by mouldings running along the edges of the

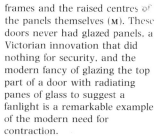

frames and the raised centres of the panels themselves (M). These doors never had glazed panels, a Victorian innovation that did nothing for security, and the modern fancy of glazing the top part of a door with radiating panes of glass to suggest a fanlight is a remarkable example of the modern need for contraction.

Windows

Sash windows had already made their appearance in important houses well before the start of the eighteenth century. They were then becoming standard in London terrace houses, but they still took much longer to reach the countryside, and then did so in a desultory way.

Early sashes were built flush with the exterior brickwork, allowing the full width of the frames to be exposed. The grooves in which the sashes slid often contained hinged props which supported the sash in either an open or closed position (A). When pulleys, cords and counterweights were introduced to make sashes open more easily, the frames were made wider so that they could contain the weights (B). This was seen as a fire hazard and the London Building Act of 1709 required the frames to be set back by the width of a brick, that is by $4\frac{1}{2}$ inches (c).

The Act may have been responsible for windows being set back in inner London, where it applied, but fashion came into it as well. A recessed window frame made a wall immediately look more solid, and emphasized the window openings in a very satisfactory way.

The 1774 Act went one stage further, and required the frames to be rebated into the inner face of the wall, so hiding them almost entirely (D). This brought the glazing bars into prominence. They helped to determine the window's proportions and the proportions of the individual panes of glass, which were all part of the reigning classical fashion. When the glazing bars are removed and the panes are replaced by plate glass, the window not surprisingly loses its character and looks empty.

Window heads

At the start of the eighteenth century, windows could have either flat or slightly curved heads, sometimes one type on one floor, the other on the next. By the middle of the century, flat heads had become far more popular, but curves came back again, especially in semicircular headed windows, and they remained popular, particularly on the ground floor of a house when they could pick up the lines of an adjacent entrance door and its fanlight (E).

A late eighteenth-century house facing Blackheath (F) in south-east London is notable for the way the entrance on the left-hand side and the windows in the middle and on the right have been assembled into a symmetrical composition, with a blank arch over the right-hand window. This balanced the fanlight over the front door and was a popular device at the time.

Occasionally a window that needed emphasis would have one of these arches, perhaps filled with decoration, or, more usually, it would have an ornamental surround in the form of an architrave (G), a motif common in grand houses, but was to come into wider use as the Victorian era approached in the 1830s.

Provincial style
The world of fashion was one thing, the provinces another. Here tradition maintained a stronger grip on style. Often sash windows took the place of older mullioned windows in an attempt to bring a house up to date. This happened so widely that it no longer looks odd, although a bad fit makes sash windows clearly inappropriate on occasion. A farmhouse at Clitheroe in Lancashire manages to have the best of both worlds. The substitution of sashes in the upper – and lesser – windows even suggests that the old-fashioned casements set beside the front door in their mullioned and transomed frames were always thought superior (H).

On the Pennines, a sturdy independence remained the rule, and bands of small windows with closely set mullions (I) stayed in use right into the nineteenth century. They were particularly necessary because the requirements of domestic weaving made good, even lighting a necessity.

G

H

I

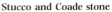

Details and decoration

The main trend in the decoration of the exterior of the Georgian house was the reduction of wood in favour of stucco and ironwork. There were two main causes for this, the first being the desire to reduce the amount of combustible material; the second was the ability to reproduce decorative forms by casting them from moulds. This was a reflection of wider advances brought about by the Industrial Revolution which allowed mass-production to become a reality.

Stucco and Coade stone

The wooden cornices that characterized houses at the start of the eighteenth century (A) were suppressed by a combination of law and taste. Brick and stone parapets took their place (B). The same process changed entrances. Here stucco and Coade stone, a form of fired earthenware, came into their own. Once a carver had produced a mould, its craftsmanship could be reproduced for as long as there was a market, and no one had a greater market than Eleanor Coade for her rusticated surrounds and keystones decorated with heads (C).

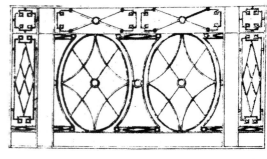

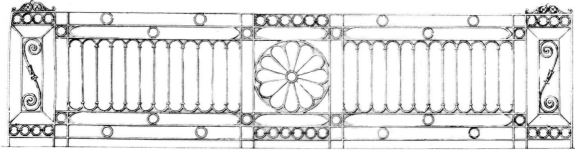

Ironwork

Wrought iron already had a long history in architectural decoration, but as the process of casting iron cheaply in standard moulds became available, the amount of decorative ironwork increased dramatically. Here, as in so many other things, pattern books showed what was possible (D), although any builder worth his salt could see the immense variety of ironwork available for railings, lamp-holders, and, above all, for window balconies. The spearhead railings at Royal Crescent, Brighton (E), complement the shiny black of the mathematical tiling.

Many railings were removed early in the Second World War, supposedly to help the war effort, but the metal was unsuitable for any purpose but railings, and they were dumped at sea to avoid embarrassment. The survivors are worth protecting; they form the best possible protection to the front of a house (F), and are not hard to replace, even though they are no longer as relatively cheap as once they used to be. At all events, they are far more attractive than the pressed and welded steel railings that sometimes take their place.

This is equally true of balcony railings (G), and even such things as cast-iron porches (H) that imitate wooden trelliswork for the sake of a rustic touch.

Privies

Most town houses had a closet where chamber pots were stored until the servants emptied them. In crowded towns this caused great problems. Many towns and suburbs followed the practice general in the countryside of having a privy built over a cess pit. This was not a particularly healthy way of going about domestic hygiene, but it provided a better alternative to overflowing gutters in the street.

The advent of mains drainage, a reliable water supply, and, with them, the water-closet, have made the privy a thing of the past. Even so, many survive, especially in the north where the Industrial Revolution brought a great expansion of towns and villages with little advance in hygiene to compensate for this. A group of communal privies behind a short terrace of weaving cottages at Rawtenstall in Lancashire (BELOW) was converted into a wash-house, but it could easily be restored to its original state for devotees of Georgian life.

Terrace house interiors

This section through an early eighteenth-century terrace house (RIGHT) shows how the passage leads from the front door to the staircase at the rear. On the way, it passes the doors of the front and back rooms. The passage, like the rooms of the floor above, is fully panelled, and an archway divides it into front and rear parts.

The ground and first floors contained the principal rooms of the house, hence the panelling, while the remaining rooms were reserved for sleeping or for the use of the servants. Consequently their walls were only plastered or limewashed, and in the attic, only took the form of the flimsiest of partitions.

A stairway leads down to the basement and a cellar under the front of the house, which has a coal hole beneath the pavement. The basement was entirely devoted to stores and cooking, and here the servants spent most of their working lives.

The staircase leads from the entrance passage up to a half landing with a closet opening off it in a small back extension to the house. A second flight then leads up to a full landing, with doors to the rear room, and to the front room, which runs right across the house. In the centre of its further wall there is a fireplace with a classical surround comprising an architrave, a bolection (or bulged) moulding for a frieze with a panel in the centre, and a cornice forming a shelf over it. Each side of the fire there are the doors of shallow cupboards.

The rooms in the storey above are simpler and were probably used as bedrooms, and the even simpler rooms above them would almost certainly have been for servants. The front room has a fireplace, perhaps for a head servant, but the other rooms in the attic are very small and only have the comfort of what warmth comes up the stairs.

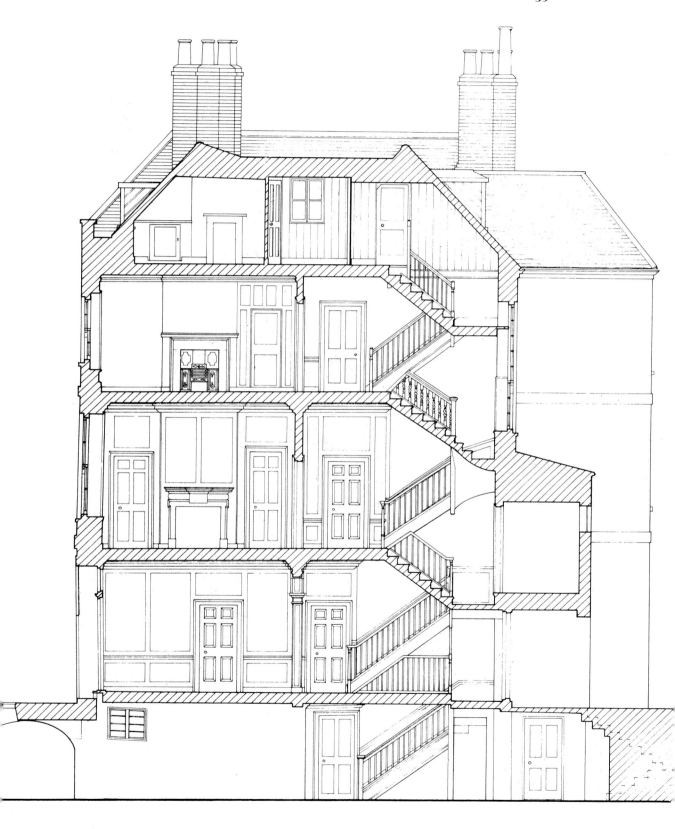

Walls and ceilings: panelling and plaster

The eighteenth century began with fully panelled walls. These now reflected classical ideals and were arranged to suggest a plinth, pilasters and entablature (A). Chimney surrounds, curved recesses for shelves, and cupboards with doors, made up the most ornate of the walls, while doors and windows fitted into other ones. By the middle of the century, such ornate timber panelling was a thing of the past. Grand rooms might still be panelled, but much of it was made from plaster, leaving dado rails and door frames made of wood, and chimney surrounds made of stone, often marble or various substitutes for marble (B).

Cornices

While dado rails remained for some while and skirting-boards have lasted until the present as vestiges of this panelling, the main decorative feature to continue was the cornice. Wooden box cornices went out of fashion soon after wooden panelling was abandoned because plaster cornices were easier to make. Temporary runners were set near the top of

continued on page 143

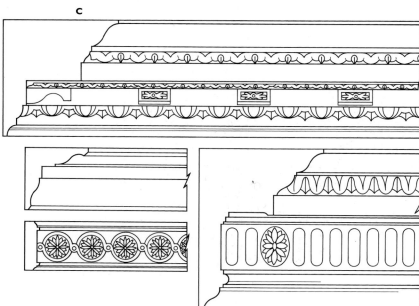

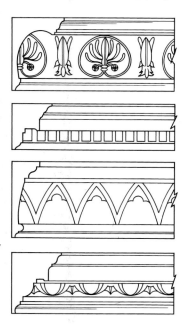

Lesser merchants and professional men lived in terraces, the most commonly built form of house in the eighteenth and nineteenth centuries. The north London suburb of Islington is famed for its terraces of elegant houses set in spacious streets or lining formal squares such as Gibson Square shown here. The houses are not particularly large, however; with basement and attic, there are eight fair-sized rooms, enough for a family and two or three servants. Because the entrance leads into a narrow passage to give as much room as possible for the front room on the ground floor, the doorway has to be squeezed against the party wall. The window beside it has to be placed centrally in the front room, with the result that they do not line up with the pairs of windows in the wider rooms above. To hide this, the ground floor is stuccoed and cast-iron balconies decorate the upper windows, thus drawing a line between the two storeys.

The same difficulty can be seen at this Georgian house in Old Steine, Brighton (RIGHT), refronted by local architect, Amon Wilds, in about 1820. He gave the front an elegant bow in the most up-to-date fashion and, because the house is wider and has three windows, not two like the houses in Gibson Square, only the front door itself is out of line. Again a balcony hides this, but here the stucco is treated differently, with channelling to provide a firm base for the attached classical pilasters that embrace the top three storeys. Instead of the normal volutes of the Ionic order, newly discovered fossils of ammonites form the basis of the decoration of the capitals, surely a reference to the architect's forename, and used by him on other houses nearby.

The kitchen fireplace of the Bailiff's House at Park Farm, Shugborough (BELOW) has a grate for coal with hobs each side, and a battery of pots and pans and a kettle ranged about it. Beside the hearth is a warm, dry cupboard where flour, salt, spices and tea could be kept. By 1800 tea was ousting beer as an everyday household drink, so much so that within a generation cottagers no longer brewed their own beer. They soon forgot how to brew, a fact bewailed by that champion of the common man, William Cobbett. He believed that tea not only led to a general enfeeblement but, for women, was a first step to prostitution.

continued from page 140

the wall, plaster was pressed into the angle and a template run along it until the cornice was fully shaped. It could then be enriched with precast ornaments, such as modillions or patera, or any of the countless other forms belonging to the classical repertoire. When they no longer pleased jaded tastes, there was Gothic, Chinese and Hindoo, and yet more exotic styles (c. page 140).

Cornices of any age are usually partly lost under layers of paint. If they are to appear as crisp as they first did, they need to be carefully stripped (D). Then the original colour may become visible, and sometimes there is evidence of gilding as well. Stripping down a cornice is a long, arduous job, but the results can be surprising (E).

Only the grander houses had ornamental plasterwork ceilings. These comprised geometrical patterns with raised rectangles and circles decorated with swags of foliage and fruit and, later, with classical mouldings such as fretwork or guilloche bands (F). Robert Adam revolutionized the plasterwork of ceilings by introducing lighter patterns suggested by what he believed was common decoration in Roman houses (G).

D

E

F

G

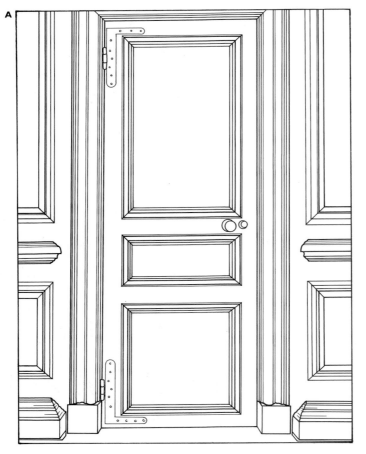

Doors and doorways

By the eighteenth century, panelled doors were almost standard indoors. The main exceptions were in secondary doorways in the servants' quarters, and in poorer houses in the countryside. Most principal doors were solidly built with panels arranged in various ways. Early in this period, door panels fitted in with the pattern of panelling in the room. Each panel was set in a raised frame (A).

When wall panelling dropped out of favour, major doors had six panels, arranged in pairs, top, middle and bottom, with the top pair wider than deep, and the lower pairs deeper than wide and roughly equal in depth. The mouldings, which might be carved, were inset from the frame, and, in the best doors, the panels might be raised and fielded (B). Later in the century, even major doors had only four panels in all, the upper ones being the taller to compensate for the loss of the small top panels. Enriched mouldings were less favoured, but they might be gilded instead. Occasionally a doorway might have a pointed head to give a room a Gothic flavour (C).

Door frames

The door frame was usually in the form of a classical architrave, and it might include some classical mouldings of the kind that surrounded the door panels, for instance egg and dart, and, later, fret or key patterns. To emphasize grand doorways, the frame might be surmounted by a frieze and cornice, and, for important doorways, there might be a pediment.

Locks

At the start of the eighteenth century, it was still common to find locks attached to the face of the door, and the lock case might be elaborately chased with floral or other patterns (D). These soon gave way to mortised locks for the most important doors with glazed porcelain or brass knobs.

Subsidiary doors were made of thinner timber and the locks, therefore, still had to be mounted on the outside. This gave some scope for a whole hierarchy of fittings. While the doors of the main reception rooms had mortised locks, the bedrooms might have theirs attached to the door, and, for the sake of status, would have brass cases and glazed porcelain knobs (E). Subsidiary rooms would have cheaper locks with iron cases and brass knobs. Meanwhile, the servants might have simple catches without locks, or old-fashioned latches, made either of iron or wood, depending on their status. The entry to the service rooms from the main body of the building, similarly, might have a good lock because the head servant and even the master and mistress of the house would pass this way.

D

E

Windows

When window frames were set flush with the exterior of the wall, and the interior of principal rooms was panelled, the inside of the window appeared in a reveal, which continued the form of the panelling. The base of the reveal could contain a small cupboard and support a convenient seat at the level of the window sill. The sides of the reveal formed a pair of shutter boxes for leaved and hinged shutters. Alternatively, a pair of shutters hung like sashes could be mounted beneath the inside of the window and rise upwards to close the window.

With window frames set back and rebated into the rear surface of the wall, and, at the same time, with the abandonment of panelled rooms, the window frame could be treated like a door frame and take the form of an architrave. The shutters would still fold into boxes set each side (BELOW LEFT). Some sash windows had side lights, making a very wide window. The shutters might then have to hinge in three places to fold away into the small space of the shutter box, but still extend far enough to cover the whole window (BELOW RIGHT).

Even well into the nineteenth century, hanging window curtains were not at all common, so shutters served the double function of making a window secure and providing some privacy after dark. They also kept cold down-draughts to a minimum. Nevertheless, with the advent of curtains, the habit of shuttering windows dropped out of fashion and shutters were often either screwed shut in their boxes or, worse, carelessly stuck fast with succeeding coats of paint – a lazy remedy for warped and sagging shutters. They are well worth bringing back into use.

Chimney-pieces

The widespread adoption of coal for the fires of most towns during the eighteenth century led to a revision of the form of a fireplace. Coal produces more heat than wood, but needs a draught if it is to burn properly, and can be smothered by its own ash. A coal fire, therefore, can be smaller than a wood one, for the same amount of heat, but it needs to be raised in a grate so that its ash can fall away. A coal fire can easily be fitted in a grate only one foot square. Few grates were over 2 feet wide and $1\frac{1}{2}$ feet deep.

Traditionally, a fireplace was the focus of a room, and so the diminution of the fire with the advent of coal made an imposing chimney-piece a necessity. The iron grate could stand in a fireplace alone, but usually it was built into a stone or tiled frame which linked it to the surround itself. Early surrounds were in the form of a stone or wooden architrave, grooved perhaps to suggest pilasters and a lintel, over which was placed a shelf (A).

These simple forms were sometimes elaborated, perhaps by the insertion of a decorative keystone and block cornice beneath the mantelshelf (B). In a really grand room the chimney-piece might extend into a full classical treatment that embraced the whole wall: the surround itself could take the form of an ornate architrave, frieze and cornice, the latter forming a mantelshelf. All this could then be framed by pilasters and an overmantel complete with an architrave of its own and perhaps a pediment as well (C).

Most eighteenth-century fireplaces had chimney-pieces based on the idea of an architrave or, otherwise, columns or pilasters and an entablature to provide the

mantelshelf. The best chimney-pieces were made of stone, and could be decorated with coloured insets and carved panels. But most were of wood, and built up, like a door frame of separate pieces, for instance for the sides and top of the architrave, for the mouldings flanking it, for the reeding of a pulvinated frieze, and again for the moulding of the cornice beneath the mantelshelf (D).

By the last quarter of the eighteenth century, these classical forms were giving way to the lighter decorative forms introduced by Robert Adam, with swags, urns and classical motifs rather than those originally used for doors and windows.

Early in the nineteenth century, these forms gave way to plain shapes, often built up from separate pieces of polished hard stone or marble, and they could be machine-cut and mass-produced for the fireplaces of rapidly expanding towns.

The soot that these fires produced brought about the Clean Air Acts of the 1950s and the change to convenient forms of heating, such as gas, electricity and central heating with water-filled radiators. Coal fires became a thing of the past, needing hard work to keep them going, as well as causing a generally condemned nuisance. Their fate, blocked to provide a mounting for gas fires or simply to keep dirt from coming down the chimney, left them as a blank reproach where once a room had its focus (E). If few people want the trouble of an open fire, even a blocked fireplace can make an attractive feature in a room if the surround is still intact.

Staircases

Towards the end of the seventeenth century, staircases still relied on heavy posts with rails supported by turned balusters rising from a closed string. These ornate forms were progressively refined in the first half of the eighteenth century, so that the staircase rapidly assumed its full role as an object of status. An open string (A) rather than a closed string (B), carved tread

ends, and turned and carved balusters with a grand newel post supporting elegant rails that swept up the staircase made it the most ornate part of a house (c).

Such staircases were only provided to link the best rooms on the principal floors, and so the staircase up to the bedrooms and, beyond that, to the attic had progressively less ornament. For instance, the main staircase might have an open string, the next flight a closed one, the two of

them with twisted and carved balusters, the attic stairs with only plain, turned balusters.

Balusters
The variety of balusters was as endless as the number of joiners willing to turn and carve them (D), and the mouldings for rails nearly as great (E). To these were added the balusters made from wrought or cast iron which graced lavish staircases. Towards the end of the century, these

forms became lighter as a consequence of the reforms of Robert Adam. Instead of turned balusters, plain square strips supported thinner rails that curled their way up a staircase (F). The carved tread ends were reduced to templates (G).

Elegance of restraint matched the times in which craftsmanship was slowly giving way to mass production, whether it was in carpentry, plasterwork, or ironwork.

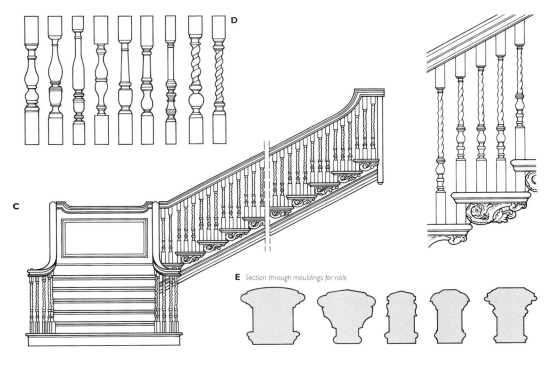

E *Section through mouldings for rails*

Victorian and Edwardian houses

By the start of Queen Victoria's reign in 1837 the house was little different from what it had been a century beforehand, except in matters of style. By the reign's end in 1901 the modern house had arrived. It had all the modern services, including mains drainage, coal-fired central heating, hot and cold running water, gas and electricity. All these made domestic life healthier and more comfortable. But this period house differed from today's houses in one important respect. It was still labour intensive, whether or not it relied on servants. The underlying class differences, both between and within households, were still expressed in its planning and detailing, which made servants second-class citizens, and might differentiate between classes of servants too, if the house were large enough.

So far as style was concerned, while the decoration of the Georgian house had become simpler and more delicate as the eighteenth century turned to the nineteenth, the Victorian house rapidly became more ornate and opulent in every way. A great variety of sources for the design of its decorative features jostled with one another for space. Classical, Gothic, Italianate, and all kinds of mannered combinations of these styles appeared everywhere. Now and then, others joined them from parts of a world coloured red on the map by trade if not by empire, to catch the imagination of people who believed that there were no boundaries on what they might achieve, just as the sun never set on the nation's possessions overseas. Before the end of the century, however, there was a partial reaction against this extravagance in the plainer forms inaugurated by William Morris and the Arts and Crafts Movement. Even then, the Edwardians are best known for their opulent tastes rather than for a new simplicity.

During the nineteenth century the terrace house remained in favour. It was endlessly adaptable in size and accommodation, so more terraces were built than ever before to house an expanding population that continued to increase until the last years of the reign. At the same time the idea inherent in the terrace, that each house was subordinated to the whole, gradually declined as individual houses were given separate features such as porches, bay windows, gables and other projections to emphasize their individuality. The plain, well-proportioned features of a terrace façade that had been accentuated by a discreet use of cast-iron and stucco details were now also put aside and condemned for their drab appearance. Some builders applied stucco ornament more liberally than ever before to their houses, but the critics, who called stucco a sham, had their way and instead builders turned to rich brickwork, enlivened with bands of different colours and cut patterns. Vigour was the key word, inside and out.

The terrace itself was not so universally admired as it had been, despite its advantages, and semi-detached houses were built in some number. They catered even better for the desire for individuality by sharing the advantages of the terrace with only one neighbour. They could be rather more expansive in plan and so needed fewer floors. They might dispense with the basement and attic and confine the servants to the rear. The semi-detached house provided the great advantage of an external side passage. This gave easy access to the rear of the house from the street at the front. It was especially useful in a small house as it allowed tradesmen to use a different entrance from the front one, which was reserved for the master, his family and visitors. It also facilitated the collection of refuse from the rear.

Garden suburbs
While the terrace still remained the norm, its obviously urban qualities were disliked by those who recognized how filthy towns had become, not just through overcrowding and insanitary conditions, but also through the tons of soot which belched through their chimneys into a once clear sky. The countryside increasingly appealed to these people as an ideal of cleanliness, health and sobriety. From this romantic idea the garden suburb was born.

Picturesque cottage estates had come into existence in the eighteenth century when rural landlords wished to improve the living conditions of their tenants. Then, early in the nineteenth century, the architect John Nash designed the two Park Villages close to Regent's Park as picturesque model suburbs with individual houses irregularly laid out in a rural manner. They were a special case, and it was not until efficient and speedy public transport made suburbs a reasonable place for city workers to live that they came into their own. So it was only in the 1870s that this idea could be fully exploited. The arrival of the garden suburb was heralded by Bedford Park in west London. Here a more self-conscious revival of past styles of architecture and a mixture of terraced, semi-detached and individual houses brought a pleasing irregularity to purposefully leafy streets.

Even then the idea of the model suburb designed with health in mind did not take immediate root. It was expensive to achieve, and it had connotations of aestheticism and radicalism which made it suspect. So, only at the start of the twentieth century did the ideal of *rus in urbe* – the countryside in the town – inspire the first true garden suburbs, notably Dame Henrietta Barnett's Hampstead Garden Suburb, and the cottage estates of the London County Council and a few other radical housing authorities. In every sense they brought a breath of fresh air to a difficult problem. Their romantic use of tradition was a typically English response to the new problem of mitigating the worst effects of industrialization on housing – and it proved to be very expensive.

At all events, this late Victorian and Edwardian coda to the story of the period house was in direct reaction to the heavy opulence of the High Victorian house. In its revivalism, it seemed to bring the story of the English house full circle, but it nevertheless provided the point of departure for the best housing of the twentieth century, and a fashion that was eventually taken up by the cheapest.

Victorian opulence

If the early Victorian house was still dependent on Regency taste for its detailing, and therefore was light and elegant, and even diffident in its decoration, this was swept aside within twenty years by a show of affluence that touched every part of the home. The diffidence of the past was now seen as drab, if not downright cheap.

On the outside, windows, doorways and porches were encrusted with stucco mouldings, mass-produced in the builder's yard. Red, yellow, grey and black bricks contrasted with coloured and shaped roof tiles, and the railways brought them into London, into every provincial town and practically every village by the train load. Coloured glass fringed doorways, coloured and glazed floor tiles filled porches. All these complemented the vigorous outline of projection and recession brought about by bay windows, deep porches, verandahs and gables.

Inside, the mouldings on timber skirtings, doorways and staircases were more emphatic, just as plasterwork on cornices, ceilings and decorative arches was thicker and more florid. Chimney-pieces were again made more opulent with the use of machine-polished stones of various hues and highly patterned and coloured glazed tiles. Whole mantelpieces were cast in iron, not just their grates, and given intricate patterns that only their mechanized production could achieve with little extra cost. Even wooden chimney-pieces were machine-cut.

This was an age of unprecedented wealth, and its public celebration in the Great Exhibition of 1851 met a private response in the fittings of the home. Indeed, the Exhibition itself had courts filled with the most exotically decorated household goods and furniture, from pianos to the gasoliers that would allow the pianos to be played long after dark in a strong clear light where, before, there had only been guttering candles and fitful oil lamps.

Industrial products began to fill the home. Even the piano became a factory product, and, as a relatively cheap form of entertainment, paved the way for the radios, gramophones and televisions of today, though not yet eroding the involvement of the household. The urban family was no longer bound together as an economic unit, as it had been in its rural past. It took on formal ties, with a strong sense of moral purpose to bind it together, and this was reflected by a change in the use of the drawing-room of the middle classes and the parlour of the working classes. These became formal rooms where the family gathered, perhaps around the piano on a Sunday evening, perhaps to entertain guests. It became a shrine where family treasures were displayed, such as mementoes of holidays at the seaside, curios brought back from the Empire by the black sheep of the family, and the new photographs recording weddings and other formal occasions when the family showed its public face. At the same time the drawing-room or parlour ceased to be an everyday room. This was the case even among those working-class people who could afford a parlour, despite the tiny size of their homes, and it remained unused throughout much of the week, polished and spotless, until the next gathering.

Wealth was not celebrated simply through a display of opulence in traditional goods and fittings. The most powerful expression of the new age was in its new light fittings, its sanitary ware, and its cooking and heating equipment. The great advantage of piped gas and, later, wired electricity was that a fixed lamp bracket allowed light to be quickly brought to the darkest part of a house with little effort. Once the coiled filament light bulb and publicly generated electricity reached houses at the end of the nineteenth century, this was achieved simply by the flick of a switch. Even with gas, which was widely available in many towns throughout Queen Victoria's reign, various methods of lighting allowed a lamp to be illuminated simply by pulling a lever.

The consequences for the house plan were that the back extension could now be extended so far to the rear, even in a terrace of narrow houses, that it obscured the daylight reaching the stairs and landings. Instead, there was now adequate artificial lighting, so that back extensions could proliferate to accommodate all the innovations which industry brought to the house.

New amenities

In the past, innovations had been a source of status, but industry made them so rapidly available that no one thought to advertise their presence by making, for instance, a scullery with a water boiler or a privy with a flushing water-closet a prominent feature of the front of the house for all to see. Self-evident reasons of privacy kept the water-closet at the rear of the house, and the same was largely true of the bathroom. The water boiler had in any case been traditionally placed at the rear because it needed much dirty labour to keep it going. So it belonged to the servants' realm and there it remained. It made no difference that it was now connected to a piped water supply and served baths and basins in other rooms. Besides, the boiler was close to the coal cellar in smaller houses that lacked basements; and in larger terrace houses, where coal was supplied directly into a basement cellar through a hole in the paving before the front door, the coal could be taken to the boiler through the basement, that is through the servants' realm, with no trouble to anyone but the servants.

Baths and, even more so, water-closets were the crowning achievement of the Victorian house. The insanitary conditions of towns brought more anguish to the Victorian conscience than any other social problem, if for no other reason than that they affected rich and poor alike. The key lay in public works, with adequate supplies of fresh water and efficient disposal of sewage being at the head of the list. Much of London is low-lying, and, relying on the River Thames for both water and sewage, it had become scandalously prone to waterborne diseases by the middle of the nineteenth century. The appalling outbreak of cholera in 1848 at last brought Government action, and in 1865 led to the Metropolitan Board of Works inaugurating the finest system of sewerage in the world.

This freed the capital from a terrible scourge, and other towns followed the lead. At the same time they introduced building by-laws which generally imposed the standards of construction enshrined in the 1774 London Building Act and its successors. This ensured that houses were soundly built and, additionally, that new houses were properly served by the new utilities so that they would not endanger the health of their occupants any more than their lives and limbs.

Speculative building

By the start of the twentieth century, speculators were running up houses so cheaply and in such great quantities that the most efficient of them could afford to sell them at cost price and take their profit from the enhanced ground rent. In the ring of suburbs now surrounding the capital some six or seven miles from the centre, a soundly built and well-fitted house with three fair-sized bedrooms could be sold for as little as £200 with only a further £2 annual ground rent. Booming industrial towns and cities built likewise, with a few particular variations among them taking the place of the old traditions and local building materials which had characterized the rural houses of the past.

Such a house served Victorian propriety in never having less than three bedrooms, thus allowing parents and their male and female children all to sleep apart. It also served the needs of cleanliness, the father of morality, with the convenience of having a bathroom with hot and cold running water as well as a water-closet. For a little more than double the price the same facilities could be built into a larger house that would accommodate a middle-class family and a domestic servant or two. That meant a scullery as well as a kitchen in the rear extension and another bedroom upstairs.

The cost of this speculative housing was so low that it jeopardized the economic basis of the garden suburbs. They were more expensive, so only a desire for exclusivity or subsidized rents kept them going. Their qualities were, happily, desirable enough for them to keep their role as an ideal domestic environment.

Despite the low cost of speculative building, only the small middle class could afford to purchase houses of its own, and even then it was not common practice in towns. At the start of the twentieth century, nine families out of ten rented their homes, partly through habit, partly through poverty. After the Great War an expanding middle class, cheap land and easy mortgages together with legislation which introduced the idea of the fair rent and curbed the profits of landlords changed all that and brought about today's circumstances in which more than six families out of ten own their own houses.

At first the ideal was a new house, complete with all the new amenities of an industrial age. It referred to the past in a few details of its styling, but old houses were mainly for people who had owned their houses for generations, or they were for the poor because they were associated with slums and substandard amenities. Consequently many old houses fell at the insistence of Public Health Officers. Nevertheless, it soon became clear that there were old houses which were stately in their associations and with qualities of craftsmanship that no new house could ever achieve. Moreover they could be brought up to modern standards without losing those qualities. At the start of this century, the weekly journal *Country Life* started to show just how stately the houses of the upper classes were, at the same time as advertising smaller old houses for people of taste lower down in society. The result has been that the period house is no longer primarily seen as old-fashioned and slummy, if not actually unfit for habitation. Instead it is treasured as living history, and part of a process of adaptation that has kept the English house up to date and able to serve in all kinds of circumstances never imagined by its builders.

Technology has made up for the lack of servants in today's houses. It has not, on the other hand, displaced old standards of construction, which ensured that houses would survive for a century or so, and they are a good insurance that many old houses can last a bit longer. So far as their accommodation goes, even the mean accommodation for Victorian servants has much to be said for it when it is devoted to modern uses. The self-assurance of Victorian decoration may be a monument to cheap labour and burgeoning industrial methods, but it is a priceless reminder of the crafts that graced all but the poorest home, and which today are too expensive even for expensive ones.

Even after two world wars and all the social upheavals that they engendered, we still stand in awe of our Victorian grandfathers. Because so much of their material world survives, and because their lives are still so well documented, our picture of them is remarkably clear. It is an imposing picture, even if it is far from being entirely attractive. This has caused much Victoriana to be defaced, if only to obliterate what people saw as its uglier side. But respect for the past rather than fear of it is a better way of facing the future. To occupy an old house, therefore, should diminish no one. It might make the pleasures of today more potent.

The difficulty, in the final analysis, is that whatever choice is made in conserving a house and its contents, only the present has any validity: what has gone has gone. It is our image of the past that has the only reality. The best reason to conserve an old house is to maintain that image as a document of the past for our own spiritual solace and support. Houses are the best bridge we have for spanning the generations, forwards as well as backwards. They are our most important cultural link, and the most personal. The yeomen of Kent understood this when they started to build the first substantial houses for the occupation of large numbers of common people. They were right, and there is no reason to believe that anything has happened since to prove them wrong.

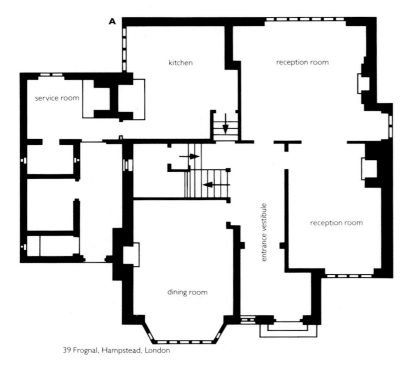

39 Frognal, Hampstead, London

Bedford Park Estate, Turnham Green

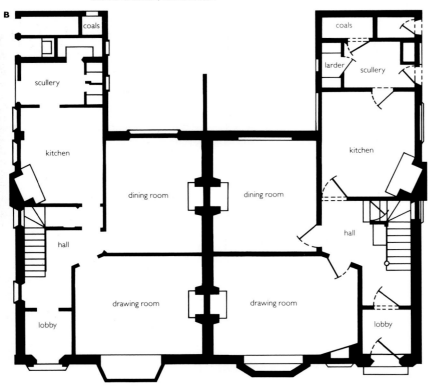

Plans

There were no radical advances in the planning of the Victorian and Edwardian house; rather, there were changes in emphasis, and these appeared mostly in its style. Never were there more styles available to architects, and never were architects more involved in designing houses.

At the start of the Victorian age, the desire for a vigorous outline greatly changed the look of a terrace of houses, but hardly changed its planning. Vigour brought an older taste for picturesque qualities to both terraces and individual houses, and again to the semi-detached house, that typically English compromise between the two older-established plans.

Queen Victoria's reign began with the double-pile plan, which was still widely used both for new farmhouses in the countryside and for villas in the suburbs. Its four symmetrically arranged rooms suited the classical taste for plain, unemphatic decoration that prevailed into the 1840s, and its comparative cheapness appealed to builders and landlords.

Victorians soon learned to despise these values, and they turned to the more ornate style of the Italian Renaissance. Industrialism and commerce were, after all, bringing a kind of renaissance to British life. The Gothic revivalist architect Augustus Welby Northmore Pugin attempted to counter this. He made everyone of taste link the moral values of the Middle Ages with the artistry and craftsmanship of their glorious abbeys and cathedrals.

This promoted Gothic with more fervour than reason as a suitable style for all kinds of buildings. On the one hand, it alone expressed the religious outlook of Queen Victoria's reign, and, on the other, it was the only style true to the materials in which buildings were constructed. It was also the only style that allowed the organization of the interior to be reflected in a picturesque ordering of the exterior. Decoration, Pugin suggested, grew out of the structure; it was not simply something added. Truth, in a number of ways, was the watchword, and only Gothic was true.

These fine ideas changed the face of architecture. The writer and art critic John Ruskin described the glories of foreign Gothic, especially the medieval brick architecture of Venice and the region around it. Much of Victorian England was built of brick, unlike medieval England, and this made Venetian practice seem especially appropriate for the times. The result was that Gothic and Italianate often came together, and sometimes in a far less holy mixture than Ruskin intended.

So hectic an attitude to style could not last, and by the 1860s architects were becoming increasingly convinced that the rigours of Gothic were not entirely appropriate for houses; the vernacular styles of the Middle Ages and the following Elizabethan and Jacobean periods might be more suitable. So it

came about that, by the end of the century, domestic architecture had settled down into a comfortable Old English style or, turning to an even later period, the so-called Queen Anne style, which mixed the medieval tradition with later motifs in the pot-pourri of styles practised around 1700.

The double pile was consequently modified and the individual rooms were expressed outside by projections and recessions (A). Porches and chimney-stacks were especially emphasized, and the roof line brought all this pleasing variety to a happy conclusion with towering stacks, tumbling gables, spiky ridges, crests and finials.

Even semi-detached pairs of houses, which formerly had been planned as though they were little different from short terraces, were now sometimes planned so that the individual houses in the pair varied (B). When the London County Council started to build working-class cottage estates in the first decade of the twentieth century, the individual cottages

had a number of different plans and were then grouped into picturesque terraces of several houses at a time.

This was a direct challenge to the widespread uniformity of working-class housing, especially in the north. Here the terrace of regularly planned houses ruled supreme. The most notorious terraces were built butting against a second terrace behind them to produce the so-called back-to-backs (c). They were often an open invitation to overcrowding and insanitary conditions, because privies could only be provided on a communal basis, and, consequently, were for everyone to use and no one to clean. Nevertheless, the best terraces of back-to-backs were solidly built and not to be despised in that they gave people sound homes which fostered community spirit. By linking backing pairs to make single houses, modern rehabilitation has turned many of them into roomy accommodation, and solved the problem of internal hygiene by making space for bathrooms and lavatories.

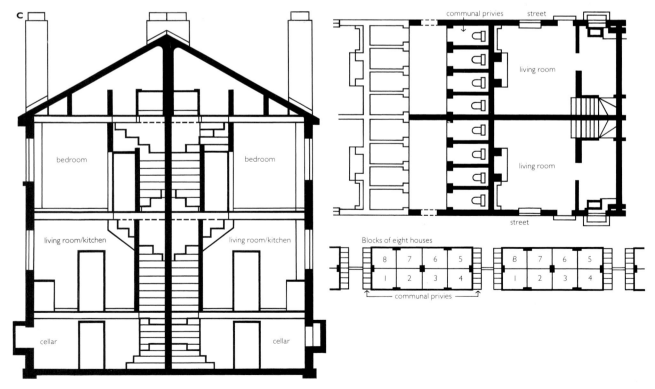

A

B

C

Elevations

The sheer variety of Victorian houses is amazing. In the past, architectural styles did not vary much in any particular place. Now, place by place, style followed style in a matter of a decade or two, and in any one place there were numberless variants. The first thirty years of Victoria's reign gave Bristol, for instance, numerous elevations for large, semi-detached houses, in which classical features gave way to Italianate ones (A).

The plain classical style that dressed the double-pile plan of many farmhouses of the 1840s soon gave way to a variety of styles, such as the Gothic of a farmhouse at Westonbirt in Gloucestershire (B), where bay windows, a gabled porch, steeply pitched roofs, and tall chimney-stacks accentuate the picturesquely irregular plan. This emphatic Gothic was a passing phase, and by the 1860s was on the wane.

Suburban villas

The same progression of styles can be seen even more sharply in suburban villas. They started the reign in the classical style of the double pile, but architects soon showed a preference for Gothic (C), and builders took it up (D). This, in turn, was ousted, or at least modified, by what dyed-in-the-wool Gothicists called 'the smirks and leers and romps of naughty 'Queen Anne'. It is

continued on page 161

D

By the middle of the nineteenth century architects could read books describing all the styles of European architecture and many others as well. It was no uncommon thing to offer houses in a bewildering variety of styles, even though some serious architects frowned on this frivolity and believed that only the Gothic style was suitable in a Christian country. When the sixth duke of Devonshire rebuilt his estate village of Edensor in Derbyshire in about 1840 the architect John Robertson offered a choice of Castellated, Swiss Chalet, Italianate and Gothic as well as Norman, shown here.

The plainest Georgian style remained common for workers' cottages such as these in Parkview (BELOW), built to accommodate the workers at James Chadwick's cotton mill at Eagley, near Bolton in Lancashire. Nevertheless, the style is not to be despised. The substitution of large-paned double-glazed metal-framed windows for the original timber sashes with small panes and glazing bars, detracts from the stylish appearance of some of these houses.

This style soon became available for poorer people, and, well before the Great War, had been adopted by the newly created London County Council for its estates of workers' cottages (RIGHT). There was a wide belief that this rural style was the most appropriate one to provide a healthy atmosphere for the industrial workers who, the authorities hoped, would come here from their crowded and insanitary slums. Unfortunately, the houses, though small, were very expensive to build and so the poorest people could not afford to pay both the rent and the cheap fares for the journey back into town where they worked.

continued from page 158

exemplified by the architect Richard Norman Shaw, in one of his Hampstead artists' houses (E).

The Gothic villa, perhaps not surprisingly, was far less successful than the 'Queen Anne' or 'Old English' one. Far better than Gothic, they epitomized a sentimental attachment to rural values (F), and, as a result, maintained an unchallenged position in the most fashionable suburbs for the fifty years before the outbreak of the First World War. They served in large villas (G) and small (H) in old suburbs like Blackheath, and in a plainer, rather more rural form – more 'Old English' than 'Queen Anne' – in new suburbs, particularly *the* suburb, Hampstead Garden Suburb (I).

E

F

G

H

I

Terraces and semi-detached houses

Large detached houses and the smaller villas were at the forefront of house design in the later nineteenth century, leaving terraced and semi-detached houses to follow, with as little or as much style as was needed to sell them.

The progression from classical through Italianate to Gothic, first English Puginian, then Venetian Ruskinian, then to 'Queen Anne', can be followed anywhere that saw speculative building continuing on even a moderate scale between 1840 and 1914. No builders used these styles as their promoters would have liked. Indeed, Ruskin was broken-hearted at the travesties of his beloved Venice that sprung up around him in south London. New elements were mixed with old, or simply misunderstood and cheapened, but they served their purpose. Consumers took to the new houses, as they had to the fashionable classical style of terraces after the Great Fire of London, but with the difference that the consumer was now far more numerous.

Gothic style

At first the plain classical designs of the 1830s were embellished by great quantities of stucco ornament, usually in an Italianate style (A), and by the 1850s this was almost standard with more or less stucco, depending on individual preference. But stucco was false, the Gothic moralists proclaimed, so some builders relied on complicated window frames, bracketed eaves and projecting porches instead, and restrained the amount of stucco (B). Other builders went further in Ruskin's direction and gave their houses Gothic porches and arches of multi-coloured brickwork of a type inspired by Ruskin's account of Venice, although never to be found there (C).

By the 1880s this sharp Gothic had settled down into the widespread elevations (D) that combined bay windows, inset porches, a little colouring from contrasting red bricks set among yellow, or yellow bricks set among red. Red ridge tiles were mixed with grey Welsh slates, and, particularly to Ruskin's dismay, some mass-produced stucco ornament nodding in the direction of the breathtaking capitals of the Doge's Palace, the 'central building' of Ruskin's world.

This Gothic did not have it entirely its own way, and for brief periods other styles made an appearance, such as the French Renaissance style, which had been popularized by the extension of the Louvre in the 1850s, and, then, from the 1860s onwards, slowly permeated taste in Britain (E). By 1900, 'Queen Anne' had been superimposed on all this, and many houses became a treasure trove for seekers of style.

Northern taste

What the speculative builders of the south and Midlands achieved was slowly reflected in the styles of those who built for mill workers in the north. Their terraces were as plain as their houses were small, and the back-to-back houses were similar. When built near fairly isolated mills, houses like these on the northern outskirts of Bolton could be attractive, and so they remain, especially when renovated – even if too thoroughly where their windows are concerned (F). Some benevolent mill owners built their houses for their workers in the moral Gothic style of the day, notably at Akroyden and Copley, near Halifax.

Leeds built back-to-back houses for as long as any other city, and streets of them remain today. They may not be where aspiring, upwardly mobile people would first think of living, because they have little or no garden, nor a yard, but a backing pair brought together can provide both spacious accommodation and some style (G).

Queen Anne style

Meanwhile, terraces outside fashionable Hampstead and Bedford Park eventually took to the 'Queen Anne' style, as did these houses close to Blackheath (H). By the start of this century,

F

G

H

I

architects were turning their full attention to housing for the working classes. Their ideas centred on the garden suburb and various forms of terrace since these were still the cheapest way of building houses. So, plainer versions of the 'Queen Anne' and

Old English styles were employed shortly before the Great War on working-class cottage estates such as the one the London County Council built at White Hart Lane, Tottenham (I), and at Hampstead Garden Suburb, where expense was less of a deterrent.

Porches

For all their vigorous decoration and moral insistence on the superiority of some styles over others, the Victorians were practical people. This showed in the entrances to their houses. An entrance needed to be seen, it needed to protect people waiting to enter a house, and it needed to impress them with its ranking. The house of a mill worker had no porch, but one step, and a small recess for the front door, protected it from the weather. The best houses had projecting porches instead, and, for all of them, this was where the style of the house was at its most lavish.

In the 1840s porches were formal and classical (A), as they had been for a long time, or informal and rustic (B) in a

picturesque way, even though both styles of porch might lead to identical types of houses; it was a matter of taste. The steeply gabled porch of the Ruskinian phase of the Gothic revival (c) was again a matter of taste, soon to be displaced by a more welcoming, flatter and wider porch in the 1870s. Sometimes these ran between projecting bay windows, continuing their roof lines in one broad sweep to provide porches for pairs of houses (D).

Posts with turned decoration, reminiscent of the seventeenth century, and characteristic of the 'Queen Anne' style, set beneath a short span of projecting roof in the form of a pentice, perhaps linked to a bay window, demonstrated the latest taste once more, and admirably kept off the rain into the bargain (E).

D

E

Entrance doorways

Projecting porches need a front area or garden if they are not to impinge on public space. A recessed porch is more urban in character, and so was far more common, since, in the nineteenth century, the vast majority of new houses were built in crowded towns.

Stucco decoration

Early Victorian entrances started with the plain classical surround of the late Georgian period, but soon builders used stucco for heavily enriched classical doorways with an Italian, French or Jacobean flavour. Ruskin's descriptions of the incised stonework that he had seen in Italy inspired many builders to produce a peculiar mixture of Italian Gothic and Renaissance styles such as was never to be found in Italy (A).

Ruskin's influence really came into its own with the Gothic terraces of the 1880s, although it was now thirty years and more since his accounts of Italy had first been published. Capitals, liberally decorated with stucco lily leaves and other foliage, became builders' stock-in-trade (B), and there were many variations. The interior of the recess often had decoratively tiled walls, here as much influenced by Pugin, a great advocate of tiles. They also had the practical advantage of keeping mud and water from boots and umbrellas from making a permanent mess. The floor as far as the front step could also be tiled (C).

Some builders favoured particular types of doorway to characterize their estates. On Archibald Cameron Corbett's estates in Eltham, Hither Green and Ilford, the entrances usually had stucco arches, round below and pointed above, that carried tall keystones bearing a mask of a god on one house (D) and of a goddess on the next.

Glazing

Even when the surround to the recessed entrance had vaguely classical stucco decoration, the front door itself might lean in a Gothic direction. By the middle of the nineteenth century, it was common for front doors to have their upper panels glazed, an advantage in that the entrance passage was better illuminated, but less good for security. The glass was often frosted so that it would hide the interior from inquisitive eyes; but various lines of coloured glass soon found greater favour both in the door panels themselves and in the fanlight overhead (E).

The front door glass might simply be in plain panels (F), or it might take on a semblance of Gothic tracery (G). Panels of coloured glass, sometimes with repeating motifs, made a frame for a small figurative centrepiece (H), or, instead, for the number of the house. All in all, the glass added to the rich, even sombre glow of colours which the Victorians admired, and kept strong sunlight from penetrating the interior and fading it all. Victorians could not tolerate drabness.

Brick and terracotta

By the last decades of the nineteenth century, the 'Queen Anne' style was appearing everywhere, from council housing to the estates of the artistically conscious. The Gothic style, it was now generally agreed, was hardly a proper style for a century that had embraced the wonders of industrialism, and the immense profits that went with it; even less was it appropriate for the twentieth century.

Exactly why 'Queen Anne' should be better was never explained, except that it had the breath of youth about it and recalled the years of greatness when Newton uncovered the secrets of the universe and Wren matched this with his enlightened architecture. So entrances took on much of his style (I), cut and moulded brick and terracotta replaced stucco, and wooden bracketed porches returned after an absence of 150 years (J). In the nineteenth century, style really did go round and round, and it continued in this way until the First World War.

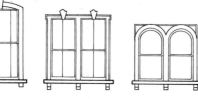

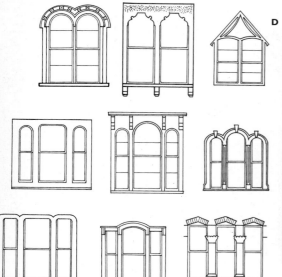

Windows

There were to be no new types of window in the Victorian and Edwardian period, but their appearance nevertheless radically changed. Thanks to advances in production initiated by the design of the Crystal Palace for the Great Exhibition of 1851, large panes of glass came into common use. Therefore fewer glazing bars were needed to hold these panes since a single sheet of glass could now be made large and strong enough to fill a sash window almost completely (A).

Had the Victorians wanted their interiors to be brightly illuminated, these new panes of glass would have been a great blessing, but colours fade in too much light, and the new windows were therefore often shaded (B). These large windows eventually did without all their glazing bars, and so became blank and characterless. As a result, more and more emphasis was placed on their frame. The number of patterns, decorated with fancy brickwork or stucco, was endless (C). A brick or stucco surround to contrast with the entrance (D and E) or to match it (F) was a widespread answer, and the characteristic use of bay windows canted out from the front was a trademark of the Victorian terrace house (G).

All this was alien to the 'Queen Anne' style, where sweetness mellowed light. It became common practice, consequently, to fill the lower sash with a single pane, and the upper one with contrastingly small panes and thick glazing bars (H); a similar arrangement put small panes in an opening fanlight and a single large pane in the space below it (I).

This was nothing like the practice at the end of the seventeenth century, but at Hampstead Garden Suburb (J) and on a few other estates, such as those built by the London County Council in the years before the Great War, sashes with a full complement of well-proportioned glazing bars became the rule. Needless to say, when these windows lose their glazing bars, or, worse, when they are replaced by modern double glazing with flush-fitting aluminium frames, the entire effect is ruined.

Where the Victorians really differed from their predecessors was in their liking for variety. Thanks to Pugin, they believed that the internal arrangements of their houses should show on the outside. It was more truthful than forcing everything into a classically ordered pattern. They learned to make wonderful compositions out of the shapes of the windows of their principal rooms, entrances, closets, staircases and bedrooms.

E

F

G

H

I

J

Exterior ornament

The vigour of the Victorian age was expressed in all kinds of ornamental detail from multicoloured bands of brick to decorative chimney-pots. Preformed stucco ornament vied with cast-iron to give a house points of interest in every direction.

Brickwork

Even modest workers' houses were decorated with courses of different coloured bricks, and nothing looks worse than when this has been obliterated by a coat of paint in the name of good taste – that is a later, unsympathetic taste. It is harder to suppress moulded brick

and carved stone, both of which became popular forms of decoration, especially about the windows (A) and eaves. Moulded or, better, intricately carved reveals to windows, and bracketed sills (B), gables hung with fish-scale tiles and finished with crested ridge tiles or fantastic terracotta finials (C); and bargeboards (D) added to an effect which encouraged the eye to dance all round the façade to wonder at the wealth it displayed.

Cast-iron

Cast-iron became more intricate as it became cheaper. Front railings and gates, balusters and rails for steps and areas, and curly balcony rails all followed Georgian

precedent, but then became increasingly ornate. Foundries sprang up in every locality to serve the building trade. None was more successful than William McFarlane's Saracen Foundry in Glasgow. From 1851, it promoted cast-iron details in its catalogues which could be applied to every part of a building, from railings to verandahs, balconies to roof ridges. Whole conservatories and bandstands could be made up from the standard bolt-together parts on offer, and these and the whole gamut of its wares were exported to all six continents.

The exhibition of 1862 brought together ornate designs for everything. Cast-iron was no exception, and balusters and

A
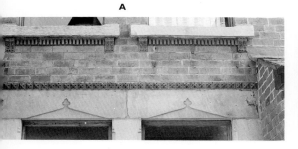

B

C

D

E

balcony rails in classical, Gothic and Italianate took their place alongside many other products demonstrating art applied to industry. Any house of pretension had a little cast-iron, if only for a balcony (E) or bay window, as it might have done in the past, but a roof crest to add to ridge tiles and decorative chimney-pots was a novelty (F).

Chimney-pots

Chimney-pots came into limited use in the eighteenth century as a means of helping the wind draw smoke out of a chimney-stack rather than blowing it back. The nineteenth century applied all its powers of invention and decoration to making them both

more efficient and more attractive. The Staffordshire potteries turned out more than the nation's crockery and fine chinaware. Among other domestic products were earthenware pipes and sanitary ware, and, capping it all, chimney-pots (G).

Designs were classical or Gothic to suit all tastes. Classical pots, rectangular and panelled, were distantly based on Roman forms, particularly on funerary monuments, as though the incinerated ashes of Roman citizens had some connection with Victorian fires (H). Gothic pots were known by their spiky tops, or the Tudor panelling of their sides. Victorian technology was represented by louvered tops

which acted as wind guards and kept out the rain (I).

All in all, the Victorians left us an embarrassing legacy with their fires. Soot filled the air, made everything filthy, and killed people in droves. This problem was at last tackled in the 1950s, so the open fire is now largely a thing of the past, and the chimney and its pots are redundant. Some people take them down, but that emasculates the roof line; others remove the pots and put a curved ridge tile over the top of the flue to keep out the rain. Thankfully, a mushroom-shaped cap fitted into the top of a pot keeps out the rain and the flue properly ventilated. It is advisable to have the chimney swept first.

F

H

I

G

Chimney-pieces

Just as the Georgians bequeathed their chimney-pieces to the Victorians and Edwardians, they in their turn bequeathed their chimney-pieces to the present day. When Clean Air Acts in the 1950s encouraged people to turn to other forms of heating which made open fires redundant, they tended to keep their Georgian chimney-pieces because the Georgian style was fashionable. Victorian chimney-pieces were another matter. They were unfashionable in the 1950s, and so they were often swept away. Others were boxed in, and gas fires put in their place. The result is that good Victorian chimney-pieces are almost as hard to find today as Georgian ones.

In the 1830s, for chimney-pieces as for other things, a plain classical style was popular. A chimney-piece might comprise a simple marble or stone surround with fluted sides representing classical pilasters, supporting a lintel with decoratively carved blocks at its ends, perhaps, with a carved panel at its centre as well.

These forms became more elaborate as the reign progressed. Heavily scrolled brackets might support an overmantel, and decorative tiles line the cast-iron grate (A). Inserted panels of different types of stone set in moulded surrounds often enriched the sides and lintel, while a round-arched grate added to the overall Italianate effect.

A chimney-piece of this type, further enriched with carving and gilding, appeared at the 1862 International Exhibition (B). This was a fruitful source of contemporary design, not least for Italianate chimney-pieces, for instance one laden with mouldings and brackets for plinths for ornaments (C), and another, highly carved one, more specifically cultured, evoking Shakespeare's *A Midsummer Night's Dream* (D). Other forms, ever more opulent (E), showed the way to more mundane suppliers who provided mass-produced wooden chimney-pieces with classical mouldings formed into an enriched architrave, set in a moulded frame with a cornice and shelf above (F).

If they were made of good enough wood with an interesting grain, the chimney-piece would be simply varnished. Cheaper wood was painted and grained to simulate a better quality. By the end of the century, these inevitably sombre colours were lightened. Grey-greens became popular for a while, and eventually white made its appearance, even though it showed the dirt and was hardly suitable for a fireplace.

The alternative Gothic style was less successful for chimney-pieces, perhaps because most medieval houses had open hearths, castles had only simple chimney-pieces, and the real monuments of Gothic, cathedrals, had none at all. Nevertheless, the forms used for chantry tombs had inspired the chimney-pieces of grand houses in the later eighteenth century, and continued to do so when Gothic became mandatory for people of highly moral taste (G). Gothic was never widely taken up, although its flavour imbued several designs at the 1862 exhibition (H and I).

The 'Queen Anne' style

returned for its inspiration to the chimney-pieces that were current around 1700, with classically decorated architraves. The desire for novelty nevertheless brought forth new shapes. The forms of the past were recast, perhaps in a sweetly sentimental way with discreetly swathed figures as supports and playful children gambolling among trees across the top; there might be touches of classical and Gothic, and bold motifs, such as a line of carved daisies (J and K), displayed in the centre. By the end of the century, there was a growing emphasis on tiled chimney-pieces, as well as tiled surrounds to the grate, a sensible development in view of the heat and dirt surrounding a fire. The inspiration here came from the artist William de Morgan, who supplied designs for tiles to be used on many chimney-pieces as well as elsewhere in the house (L).

Floors

There was little advance in Victorian England in the way that houses were floored. Boards were invariably used for floors except in the basement, where stone flags remained common. Occasionally a well-built house might have the boards tongued and grooved, a luxury that made the floor marginally firmer and reduced the penetration of dirt.

For the first time in comparatively modest houses, the boards might be designed to be seen, in which case they could be laid with panels of different wood to form contrasing borders. On a firm floor, blocks of wood might be laid in patterns, with squares, stars and roundels set within borders. The most common pattern for these parquet floors was a simple herring-bone made from rectangular blocks.

Tiled entrances again became fairly common. The Staffordshire firm of Minton made a name for itself in the middle of the nineteenth century by paving the new Houses of Parliament and numberless Gothic Revival churches with glazed tiles decorated with medieval patterns. These patterns were occasionally applied to houses, but Italianate patterns became more popular, and whole floors were on offer decorated to suggest luxurious Roman villas (BELOW), sometimes even bearing the messages 'SALVE' and 'VALE' to encourage the classically educated.

Plasterwork

As in all other matters of style, Victorian plasterwork elaborated on the forms of the Georgian era. Plaster arches dividing entrance passages from staircases, plaster cornices and the centrepieces that now might surround the hanging point for a gasolier all abandoned the plain, understated classical forms of the earlier nineteenth century, and looked to the luxuriance of a more Italianate style, or, occasionally, adopted the spikiness of Gothic. As with chimney-pieces, there was little medieval precedent for Gothic cornices, so Tudor was tried instead. When the 'Queen Anne' style finally became popular, the mixed Renaissance forms of the seventeenth century came with it.

Walls and ceilings

The walls of passages and staircases were increasingly protected by dados, and houses in the 'Queen Anne' style had them in their principal rooms as well. The wall beneath the dado rail was then covered in thick papier maché pressed into various patterns (A). Dividing arches were usually supported by Italianate brackets (B), often decorated with luxurious leaf forms.

Cornices were decorated with running patterns of leaves and garlands of flowers. Sprays of roses and trefoiled leaves could give a cornice a Gothic effect (C), which could be heightened by tiers of corbelled, trefoiled arches

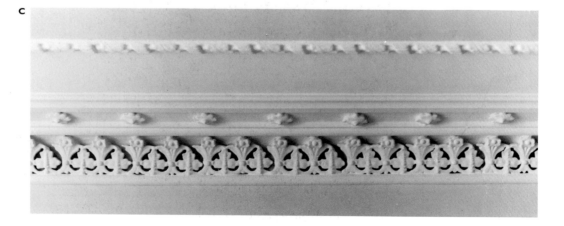

(D). Twining garlands, on the other hand, were associated with Renaissance Italy (E). By the 1870s, grand houses had very luxurious cornices indeed between the walls and ceilings of their best rooms, with a complicated web of mouldings, inset sprays of flowers, garlands and bands of foliage (F).

Circular 'roses' with similar, radiating patterns were set in the middle of the ceilings of best rooms (G), and from their centres hung the new gasoliers that brought instant light to the Victorian house.

This ornate Victorian plasterwork has suffered even more than the plainer Georgian plaster mouldings, from a build up of paint that obscures its form. This is despite the fewer coats of limewash and paint that have been applied over the years, and mainly a consequence of the greater complication and depth of the mouldings themselves.

D

E

F

G

Staircases

At the start of Queen Victoria's reign, the staircases of ordinary houses had changed very little for fifty years. An open string with template scrolls beneath the treads, plain strip balusters and a rail that leaped upwards, flight by flight, combined cheapness and elegance.

The Victorians soon reintroduced turned and carved balusters to add a little vigour to this elegance (A), and increasingly heavy, turned newel posts brought the baluster to an abrupt end (B). The staircase itself appeared much heavier because, unlike the open spaces beneath the flights that were characteristic of Georgian staircases, the underside was now panelled and cupboards were tucked into this convenient space.

The template scrolls that

decorated the tread ends were omitted, and, at the same time, the open string was abandoned and a closed string, sometimes heavily moulded, went in its place (C). This suited the 'Queen Anne' style, since closed strings were still the rule in the later seventeenth century.

Even now, the old ideas of status did not vanish from staircases, and, while the main flights might have heavily turned balusters, albeit mass-produced, the flight down to the servants' basement might have plain strip balusters (D).

Cast-iron balusters were mainly confined to grand houses, but classical, Italianate and Gothic patterns were produced by foundries and occasionally used in the staircases of smaller houses (E and F), though never as frequently as the mass of cast-iron decoration applied outside.

D

E
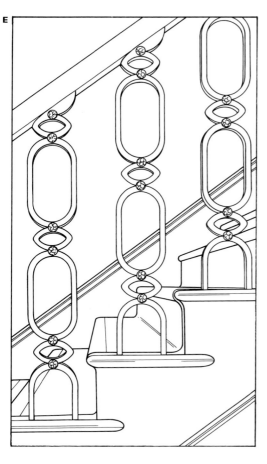

F
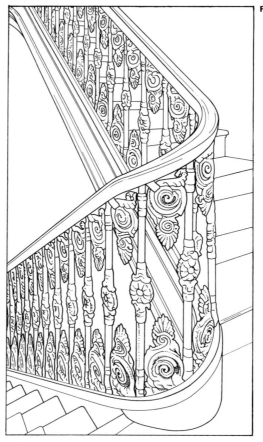

A

New amenities

Of all the new amenities
introduced into Victorian and
Edwardian houses, none promoted
health more than safe drains and
efficient sewerage. Without them,
the large-scale introduction of
piped water to individual houses
would have brought chaos. Once
they had arrived, a house could
be fitted out with baths, basins
and water-closets, and the
occupants could consume any
amount of water and dispose of it
almost without thought.

Baths and bathrooms

Water-closets were fitted into new
small rooms, the successors to the
external privy and the internal
closet. In the smallest houses they
remained out of doors, but there
was little real difficulty in finding
the space for them indoors,
especially upstairs, where they

B

C

were both convenient and easily ventilated. Bathrooms also succeeded closets and dressing rooms, but they introduced a different kind of novelty for the many people who had previously bathed more or less in public in a tub before the living-room fire. So, the bathroom was a triumph not just for health and hygiene, but for modesty as well. The two ideas became confused, leading among other things to the Boy Scout Promise 'to be clean in thought, word and deed'.

Remarkably, baths have changed very little in shape since the early days. The movable bath tub was designed for comfort and efficiency, and therefore sloped at one end to provide a comfortable back-rest. It fitted closely round the human body along its length so that it needed the least amount of water to fill it to a comfortable depth. The resulting shape was

used for fitted baths and remains today.

Early baths were sometimes embellished in a number of ways, and often mounted on elaborate feet, shaped like lions' or eagles' claws (A). But boxed-in baths appeared in grand houses and soon moved down society because they obviated the need to clean under them and could be fitted out with shelves for brushes and holders for sponges, and soap (B).

Basins and lavatories
Wash-basins developed from wash-stands, and again were provided with holders for every possible requisite (C). The design of the lavatory bowl needed more ingenuity since it had to incorporate a means of thoroughly flushing it with a trap to stop foul germ-laden air rising through it from the sewer into which it drained. By 1890 the

modern 'washdown' bowl, with an S-bend for a trap, was in use and provided manufacturers with plenty of scope for decoration (D), a feature that was quietly forgotten in the twentieth century in the belief that decoration obscured dirt, and only white was properly germ-free and hygienic.

Even the idea of the fitted *en suite* bath and lavatory unit was developed by Victorian England (E), although it did not come into common use until after the Second World War. In some of the houses which the London County Council built on its cottage estates shortly before the Great War, the fitted bath was a necessity, not for reasons of luxury, but to save space: the bathroom was placed next to the scullery, and, when not in use, the bath was covered over and became a table. All in all, the bathroom was an apt symbol of Victorian ingenuity.

The Victorian and Edwardian interior

The interiors of medieval houses were empty by today's standards, simply because most people were too poor to own much beyond what they needed for their everyday lives. Their needs were small and their lives had few physical comforts. Victorian and Edwardian interiors, by contrast, were impossibly crowded. The Industrial Revolution was increasingly making people wealthy beyond the dreams of the past, and so every room was full of furniture and fittings designed for comfort (TOP LEFT).

Possessions were also a sign of wealth, as they always had been, but the Victorians were not yet so wealthy that household goods were not treasured, and that is why the Victorian and Edwardian house was so full. A full house was almost an end in itself: just as the outside was a mass of decoration, the inside was a receptacle for pictures, vases, ornaments, trophies and all kinds of treasures that filled every corner of every room.

Today we have grown to accept the results of industrial production; obsolescence and the disposal of unwanted goods are the results. Houses less than full of bric-à-brac are another result. We no longer have the servants who can waste their lives caring for half the contents of the Victorian home, and many people cannot be bothered to do it themselves.

The changes are most evident in the kitchen, where the whole process of cooking meals was an endless labour, undertaken by mistress and servants with a continuous supply of raw materials, an immense *batterie de cuisine*, a large cast-iron range (BELOW LEFT), and shelf upon shelf of storage space, all to produce a constantly changing menu from a wide range of recipes designed to make the best of a growing range of basic ingredients.

All of that has changed. Today, one can live off packaged and processed food which needs no more than a few minutes in a

microwave oven, and even the
addict of whole food has so many
aids that the Victorian kitchen is
more an encumbrance than a
help. Ultimately, the period
kitchen is now a matter of taste,
like any other period interior,
and its wholesale conservation
produces only the museum
period piece.

The opposite view, that a house
is a machine for living in, has
always been partially accepted,
perhaps never more so than in the
past, when all houses were places
of hard and constant work, not
simply somewhere to return to for
relaxation after work. They had to
be efficient to use, and this is still
a necessity, particularly in the
bathroom and the kitchen. But it
is not an appropriate view of the
house as a whole.

Further reading

It is a great temptation when moving into a house to make immediate plans for decoration and improvement, and then rush them into effect so that the filth and inconvenience they bring is quickly over.

Such haste is fine, but it cannot be undone by repentance. An old house needs consideration before speed. It will often become apparent how little needs to be done. A house is not the same as a car. If it has survived for generations, it is unlikely to be worn out. It has already demonstrated staying power, and is likely to have plenty left. So, before any work is started, the house needs to be understood. Work needs to be undertaken with care so that plans can be altered if new evidence of the house's original form becomes clear during the process.

All this requires knowledge and understanding. Therefore the following reading list may be helpful. It takes the history of the small English house many stages further than has been attempted here, and in a number of different directions.

General books dealing with small houses are legion. They fall into two types, those that describe the various types of house in detail, phase by phase, part by part, and those that explain its historical development in a wider social and economic context. These consequently view the house less as a structure to be understood for itself than as the principal physical feature that shapes people's lives, for better or worse, and therefore to be understood as a real document of history.

The more recent general histories begin with Maurice Barley's *The English Farmhouse and Cottage* (Routledge and Kegan Paul, 1961), which covers the history of rural houses from the Middle Ages to the eighteenth century, in short periods and region by region. Medieval studies were not far advanced when it was published, and the coverage is rather disjointed, but both of these failings are remedied in his *Houses and History* (Faber and Faber, 1986), where small houses are set in the context of domestic architecture since the early Middle Ages. Much is condensed, and much is omitted, particularly after the eighteenth century; but it is the best approach to the subject. The present author's *House and Home* (BBC Publications, 1986, in association with a television series of the same name) has eight essays dealing with clearly defined subjects from the Middle Ages to the present, and, although it omits much, presents eight specific types of house in their economic and social context. More specialized histories include John Burnett's admirable *A Social History of Housing, 1815–1985* (Methuen, 1986), and the more detailed *The English Terraced House* (Yale University Press, 1982) by Stefan Muthesius.

Any list of books describing smaller houses in detail must include Ronald

Brunskill's *Illustrated Handbook of Vernacular Architecture* (Faber and Faber, revised edition 1978); its wide coverage and clear explanations make it deservedly popular. Eric Mercer's *English Vernacular Houses* (HMSO, 1975) is both very detailed and dry; it stops short in the eighteenth century and hardly deals with houses in towns. Its Welsh companion, Peter Smith's *Houses of the Welsh Countryside* (HMSO, 1975) is even more detailed, but generally easier to read. Pamela Cunnington's *How Old is Your House?* (Alphabooks, 1980) is a good introduction which answers many more questions than the one posed in the title, as well as combining some results of restoration work with many practical hints.

The classic book on building materials is Alec Clifton-Taylor's *The Pattern of English Building* (Faber and Faber, 1972), a book as detailed and as readable as his later sudies of English towns. His later book with Ronald Brunskill on brickwork is good for its descriptions but less so for its history. Timber-framing is a controversial suubject and its most controversial historian is Cecil Hewett, whose *English Historic Carpentry* (Phillimore, 1980) summarizes and corrects much of his earlier work. It is not easy to read, but this is made up for by Richard Harris's admirably brief *Discovering Timber-framed Buildings* (Shire Publications, 1979).

More specialized books deal with the houses of clearly defined regions and their details. *London: The Art of Georgian Building* (Architectural Press, 1975) by Dan Cruickshak and Peter Wyld illustrates a fashionable period and its origins: it is an invaluable source book, although Sir John Summerson's *Georgian London* (first published 1945, now by Penguin Books, 1962) is the standard history. Many other books on London add to this; and the continuing volumes of *The Survey of London* are unrivalled in their detail. Sir Nikolaus Pevsner's classic series *The Buildings of England* (Penguin, 1951, revised editions continuing) is the first source for information, although smaller houses are not its first concern. Reference libraries will have local works, and the Conservation Officer will know which are worth consulting.

The best brief, all-round coverage of the interiors of houses is James Ayres's *The Shell Book of the Home in Britain* (Faber and Faber, 1981, but now out of print), which progresses from heating and lighting to painting and wallpaper. As its title implies, Judith and Martin Miller's *Period Details* (MJM Publishing Projects, 1987) is a compendium of information about fittings from the sixteenth century to the present.

How these and indeed all aspects of old houses dating from after 1750 should be treated is thoroughly covered in *Putting Back the Style* (Evans Brothers, 1982), edited by Alexandra Artley, in which experts assess the problems of restoring the various parts of Georgian and later houses, and provide invaluable lists of craftsmen and suppliers. For these alone it is essential reading before any old house is restored. Rather more specialized in their different ways are F. W. B. Charles's *The Conservation of Timber Buildings* (Hutchinson, 1984) and Alan Johnson's *How to Restore and Improve Your Victorian House* (David and Charles, 1984). Finally, when it comes to restoration work itself and the need to find craftsmen, there is the *Guide to Restoration Experts* (Guild of Master Craftsmen Publications, 166 High Street, Lewes, East Sussex, BN17 1YE), now in its fourth edition and constantly being kept up to date.

Glossary

architrave lowest, structural part of *entablature* forming a *lintel*, or similarly formed surround to an opening

attic top *storey*, set above *cornice* in classical building

B

baluster supporting post, usually decorated, of handrail

bay vertical section of a building, sometimes divided by structural members

bower archaic word for *chamber* or private room

box-frame timber frame made up of horizontal and vertical timbers, usually also forming the walls, which supports the roof

brace triangulating piece, usually in timber-framed building

bressummer horizontal, intermediate structural timber, or timber such as supports a chimney-breast over a fireplace

buttery service room, usually for storage of bottles (Fr. *bouteille*), hence liquid foodstuffs

byre northern dialect for cattle house

C

came metal frame to hold individual panes of glass in a window

capital decorative top of column immediately beneath *architrave*

casement vertically hinged opening window

chamber private room

chamfer flattened edge

chimney-piece decorative surround to fireplace

classical style style of decoration originating in ancient Greece and Rome, much revived thereafter, depending on symmetry, proportion, and an ordered vocabulary of ornament

closet small, private room, often for storage or the intimate conduct of bodily functions

Coade stone form of fired clay, promoted and mass produced from 1769 by Eleanor Coade for decorative features

cob building material comprising a naturally dried mixture of clay, earth, sand, pebbles and binding materials such as cowhair, straw and brambles, much used in the West Country, and with different names in the north; unbaked bricks of a similar material were often used in Essex, East Anglia and many Midland counties

cornice the upper, projecting part of a classical *entablature*, designed to stop rain from running down the face of a building

cove curved piece, usually joining a wall to ceiling

cross-passage passage running across house, usually adjacent to a hall, between front and rear entrance doors

crown-post timber post rising into roof space from a *tie-beam* to support a longitudinal timber or crown-plate which carries collars linking pairs of *rafters*

cruck curved timber, used in pairs to form a bowed A-frame which supports roof of building independently of walls

D

dado *plinth*, and hence lower part of wall

dairy room used in storage and preparation of milk products

dais raised floor, usually at high end of hall further from entrance or low end

dais-beam decorative beam fixed to wall at high end of hall behind high table, sometimes as an alternative to a *cove*

daub mixture of earth, clay, sand and binding material such as cowhair or straw, often used to fill panels of timber building

dendrochronology process of dating timber by studying the differential annual growth as shown in the rings of wood laid down each year

double-pile plan plan of house usually formed by two clearly identifiable contiguous ranges, one at the front, one at the rear

dovetail reversed wedge-shaped timber joint designed to withstand tension, for instance between a *tie-beam* and a pair of *wall-plates*

dragon-post *post* at corner of a building bearing a projecting diagonal beam, usually in association with *jetties* on adjacent sides

dripmould projecting moulding designed to throw rainwater of face of building, usually as decorative as functional

E

eaves part of base of roof overhanging wall

elevation all the parts of a building facing one specific direction

entablature classical *lintel*, comprising an *architrave* or main structural component, decorative *frieze*, and *cornice*

F

fanlight window upper window or part of window, originally semicircular and decorated with radiating bars in shape of fan

firehood wide funnel shaped chimney, usually made of timber and plaster

firehouse northern word for hall

frieze horizontal band of decoration

G

gable upper part of wall rising into end of roof

galletting insertion of small chips of stone into *mortar* between larger stones to reduce amount of mortar and produce decorative effect

garret upper room, often in roof space

glazing bar support for panes of glass set within window frame

Gothic style style of architecture developed in Middle Ages depending on pointed arches, ribbed vaults and buttresses for its structure and a significantly different vocabulary of ornament from the classical style, much revived, especially in the nineteenth century, when it was associated with Christianity particularly Protestantism and imbued with moral qualities

guilloche ornament in form of braid

gutter trough, usually at base of roof, designed to catch rainwater and channel it to downfall pipe

H

hall large public room, usually open to the roof and containing a hearth, used as main living-room in Middle Ages; not to be confused with entrance vestibule in later houses

hall-house house whose main room is an open *hall*

heck northern word for a partition, usually shielding a hearth and *ingle* from a doorway or passage

hip slanting outward angle between two adjacent parts of a pitched roof, the opposite of a valley, the inward angle

I

ingle space under a firehood or beside a fireplace

J

jetty projecting *joists* extending a floor beyond wall below

joist horizontal supporting member, usually of timber to carry a floor

K

keystone centre stone or voussoir at head of arch holding it together

king-post vertical roof timber supporting a *ridge-beam*

L

landing space at top of staircase

lantern opening, usually in roof, to let in light

light well vertical opening, such as between flights of stairs, to let in light

lintel flat structural top of an opening

lobby-entry plan plan of house in which entrance is into a lobby which gives access to flanking rooms and backs on to chimney-stack set between them

loft low upper room open to roof

long-house house with shared access to living accommodation and cattle stalls

louver ventilation opening covered with slats to reduce entry of rain and light

M

milk-house dairy

modillion projecting bracket, usually supporting *cornice*

mortar mixture of sand and lime and sometimes clay used to bind bricks or stones together

mortise hole in framework, usually designed to receive a *tenon*

mullion vertical framing member of an opening such as a window

O

Old English style style developed in the nineteenth century, romantically based on the traditional buildings of the past

oriel projecting window bracketed out from wall

P

pantry store room for food, originally flour and bread (Fr. *pain*)

parapet top of wall, sometimes when projecting above roof

pargetting plasterwork, usually decorated with inscribed or raised patterns

parlour private room, descended from *chamber*, usually not for sleeping

patera flat, round ornament in classical style, like a rosette

pediment formalised classical *gable*

pentice single-pitched roof attached to side of wall

Picturesque style style developed in the eighteenth century whose effect is to recall the romantic ideals of pictures, often distinct from the classical style in lacking symmetry, proportion or order to heighten naturalistic effect

pilaster flat projection with form of a column, used to decorate and articulate a wall or pier

pitch angle at which roof slopes upwards from horizontal

plinth base, as for classical column or *pilaster*

porch projection shielding entrance from weather

post principal vertical structural timber

privy small private room, often used for excreting or emptying chamber pots into cess-pit

Pugin fervent early Victorian advocate of *Gothic* style as only true style for a Christian country and only style able to reflect the functions of a building without otiose decoration

purlin longitudinal roof timber designed to support *rafters*

Q

Queen Anne style style developed in the 1870s loosely based on mixture of traditional and classical motifs current around 1700

R

rafter   timber on to which roof covering is fixed

rail   horizontal timber, such as in a wall or door

rainwater head   hopper into which *gutter* drains

Renaissance style   classical style first revived in Italy in fifteenth century

ridge-beam   longitudinal timber running along ridge of roof to divide heads of *rafters*

Ruskin   fervent Victorian advocate of *Gothic* style, especially the colourful brick Gothic found in the region of Venice

S

sash window   window whose opening are filled, usually with a pair of vertical sliding glazed frames

scarf-joint   joint connecting the ends of two timbers

scullery   small service room

semi-detached plan   pair of houses joined together, usually so that the plan of one is a mirror image of the other

service room   room used to store goods, usually food, and prepare it for cooking

shop   room or building used for manufacture or sale of goods

shutters   moveable panels usually fitted to block windows

sill   base, for instance of wall or window

slate   specific type of impermeable stone which can be split into thin layers usually for covering roofs or making damp-proof courses

storey   floor, particularly the space between two floors

string   timber support for stair

stud   secondary vertical timber

stucco   form of patent hard plaster

style   vertical timber, as in wall or door

T

tenon   projecting piece of timber designed to fit into mortise to form a joint

terrace   row of joined houses, often similar and designed as a whole

thatch   roof covering of straw or reed or other vegetable substance

tie-beam   transverse beam linking tops of two walls designed to counter outward thrust of roof above

tile   flat baked clay or split stone slab used for roof, floor or wall covering

timber framing   structural part of timber house comprising vertical, horizontal and diagonal members rigidly joined together

tracery   decorative stonework or timberwork filling top part of opening such as a window

transom   horizontal bar set across an opening such as a window

truss   transverse structural timber frame designed to support a roof

W

wall-plate   longitudinal timber set along top of wall

Wealden hall   *hall-house* common in Kent and Sussex (not just the Weald) characterized at front by *hall* recessed under overhanging roof and between *jetties* of flanking wings

weather boarding   overlapping horizontal boards making a wall weatherproof

wing   projecting end of a building

Index